a WEALTHY *Girl*

7 Steps to Prosperity, Peace, and Personal Power

CHARISSE CONANAN JOHNSON, CFA

Net worlding PUBLISHING

A Wealthy Girl
7 Steps to Prosperity, Peace, and Personal Power

Charisse Conanan Johnson, CFA

eBook: 978-1-944027-77-3
Print: 978-1-944027-76-6

a
WEALTHY
Girl

For Gabrielle, and all the Wealthy Girls
who want to embrace their full selves.

Contents

Taking a New Wealth Journey

IMAGINE THAT YOU ARE standing in front of a mirror saying, "I am a Wealthy Girl."

How do you feel when you say these words out loud? What is the expression on your face? Do you truly believe in the power of your own words?

I have gone through this exercise myself. But I must keep it real with you—it's more than an exercise. It's who I am.

I feel free. I feel powerful. I feel affirmed. I am smiling, showing lots of teeth. I believe that the person staring back at me *is* wealthy.

If it is hard for you to imagine yourself saying these words or having the feelings that I have described, then this is the perfect book for you. If you have no issues saying these words out loud, have you checked in on your friends to see if they can do the same? By the end of this book, my deep hope is that you can say these words boldly and authentically in your own voice, and that the women around you can do so too.

Most of us want to be wealthy but, more often than not, we don't really have a handle on *how* to achieve this goal, especially in the face of the very real systemic forces that have intentionally helped some people obtain wealth and held others back because of their gender, race, sexuality, class, or a combination of any of these factors. Plenty of well-documented research forcefully concludes that America was set up to prevent certain communities from obtaining wealth. For example:

> *African-Americans living in rented apartments, prohibited from moving to the suburbs, gained none of that [housing] appreciation. The result is that today nationwide, African-American incomes on average are about 60 percent of white incomes, but African-American wealth is about 5 to 7 percent of white wealth. That enormous difference is almost entirely attributable to unconstitutional federal housing policy practiced in the mid-20th century.*[1]

MacKenzie Scott (ex-wife of Jeff Bezos, one of the world's richest men) said it best when she gave over a billion dollars in 2020 to organizations founded by women, LGBTQ persons, and the people of color who helped her generate her wealth: "There's no question in my mind that anyone's wealth is the product of a collective effort, and of social structures which present opportunities to some people, and obstacles to countless others."[2]

This book is not your ordinary wealth-building book. I will show you that you don't have to be male, rich, old, or white to be wealthy.

I am a young Black woman with Filipino roots who has amassed great wealth. But the kind of wealth that I have amassed goes beyond the prosperity that comes from a growing bank account; my kind of wealth also brings peace and personal power. I will show you how to get this kind of wealth.

I subscribe to a different, more expansive definition of wealth. I also want you to embrace this broader definition of wealth, and thus take a new wealth journey with me. It will transform your life.

Traditionally, wealth has been defined in dollars and cents. Pew Research Center defines wealth as net worth or "the value of assets owned by a family, such as a home or a savings account, minus outstanding debt, such as a mortgage or student loan. Accumulated over time, wealth is a source of retirement income, protects against short-term economic shocks, and provides security and social status for future generations."[3] In America, there is a lot of this kind of wealth. In fact, American households held over $98 trillion of net worth in 2018, derived from $113 trillion in household assets minus $15 trillion in household debt. And 75 percent of these household assets comes in the form of financial assets, namely stocks and mutual funds, retirement accounts, and privately held businesses. Of nonfinancial assets, real estate makes up the vast majority. On the other hand, two-thirds of America's aggregate household debt comes in the form of mortgages on that real estate, followed by consumer credit and student loans.[4] (If you are a millennial like me, you know how incredibly frustrating it has been to be hindered by student loan debt.)

Think of traditional wealth as your very own balance sheet, measured at a singular point in time. In a traditional sense, your wealth can go up or down over time based on changes in income, how much debt you take on or pay down, and what might have been given to you or that you give away. What you earn from your paycheck is not wealth. That's straight-up income, and I don't want you to get income confused with traditional definitions of wealth. You can have a very high income and still have little financial wealth if you spend all your money, don't save or invest, or have a boatload of debt.

When I studied economics at Yale University in undergrad and pursued my MBA at the University of Chicago Booth School of Business, I learned that this traditional type of wealth often dominates the narrative in defining us as individuals, communities, and countries and invites us to measure differences in tangible wealth between different groups.

However, defining your wealth solely in these terms misses the mark on all of the assets that you possess. Wealth must also include the very important intangible assets that include your faith, family, networks, personal attributes, and skills that make you special in this world.

Society will have you believe that the only wealth that matters is financial wealth. While I believe wholeheartedly in pursuing this kind of wealth, it's not the *only* wealth that matters. I challenge the traditional monetary-only definition of wealth because it misses the mark on who I am as a woman, as a mother, and all of the other ways in which I value myself. Defining wealth solely in financial terms misses some of my greatest assets, and it surely misses some of yours too.

I offer an expansive definition of wealth: the traditional dollars and cents version *plus* all of the intangible assets that make a person who they are. You can have all the financial prosperity in the world, and it can still fall short of generating a sense of peace or personal power. To redefine wealth as both tangible and intangible allows you to define wealth on your own terms.

My expansive definition of wealth comes from having achieved high levels of both tangible and intangible wealth over my entire lifetime. On the tangible wealth side, I have a unique set of experiences as an investor, entrepreneur, and strategy consultant over the last twenty years. From making investments for J. P. Morgan's multi-billion dollar, mid-cap value fund to helping grow Yale University's alumni venture fund to starting my own personal finance technology company, I have been on the front lines of building tangible wealth. In my twenties, I dedicated three years to obtaining my chartered financial analyst (CFA) designation so that I learned the skills necessary to make investment decisions for billion-dollar portfolios. I've learned the secrets of how to make money within traditional wealth producing structures: investing in stocks, getting passive income from real estate investments, making venture capital investments, and starting a business. I am going to share these tested strategies with you.

Over the last five years as a strategy consultant and now managing partner at Next Street, a mission-oriented, for-profit firm, I have advised some of the world's most dynamic institutions. Through my work at Next Street, I develop innovative and data-driven strategies to help close the wealth gap between the "haves" and the "have nots," using entrepreneurship as the primary lever. Whether developing these strategies for progressive foundations such as the Obama Foundation, complex financial institutions such as U.S. Bank, or forward-thinking governing bodies such as the City of Columbus, I understand how institutions and systems play a critical role in an individual's ability (or lack thereof) to generate wealth.

By being entrenched in traditional institutions as both an investor and an advisor, I have also developed a deep understanding of how best to grow traditional wealth in spite of the ways these institutions have historically and systematically prevented people who look like me from creating wealth. I am going to share concrete examples of how these systemic forces have played out, along with tested strategies to both build wealth through these systems and subvert them when necessary.

I have spent years testing and developing my own unique process to attain and sustain traditional wealth, creating a very vibrant financial status not only for myself and my family, but also for members of my Charisse Says community, where I've advised thousands of people at www.CharisseSays.com through my blogs, videos, courses, and tools. I will share all of my hacks and strategies to obtain traditional wealth.

And still I want something more for you. I want you to have more than traditional wealth. Why?

I am tired of being exclusively defined by the same systems and structures that have historically tried to prevent me, a young Black female, from fairly participating in the traditional accumulation of wealth. Most Western cultures were built on imperialist systems and structures of patriarchy, sexism, racism, and classism that have tried to put me in a box. I want to break that box wide open. Why chase a *single* standard that never entirely had me or you in mind anyway?

I want you to have the kind of wealth that goes beyond dollars and cents. Wealth must *also* encompass your intangible assets, such as your spiritual and physical well-being, emotional and mental health, education attainment (formal and informal), relationships, and cultural capital and the exposure to different cultural forms (such as art, museums, and traveling) that enhance one's social capital.

For example, spiritual well-being means building a faith muscle, which I talk about in Chapter 9. Your faith can be one of your strongest and most powerful intangible assets, which means that your faith can make you incredibly wealthy. You should know right up front that I am Christian, and my views on faith are shaped through that lens, and yet I believe that faith is accessible to all. My Christian upbringing, heavily influenced by my two grandmothers and then my parents, has formed a strong sense of purpose. I want you to experience the power of living a faith-filled life. I believe that wealth and faith go hand-in-hand, and thus being wealthy means having faith. It's more precious than rubies, gold, or, better yet, the bank's dollars.

I am a living witness to the fact that your intangible faith will give you all the desires of your heart, not just those defined by monetary gain. Isn't that why we aspire toward wealth anyway? To be wealthy certainly involves having the things we want and need.

I am also a woman who was born with strabismus (or as they say "crossed eyes"), a condition that almost caused me to go blind at a very young age. My ability to thrive academically, emotionally, and socially despite my disability created a high degree of confidence within me at a very young age. I am wealthy because I am confident, and my confidence is one of my most salient intangible assets.

I grew up in Freeport, a small, blue-collar village in Long Island, and attended public schools until college. I didn't grow up with a silver spoon in my mouth, but I do come from a community that nurtured my talent and taught me to strive for excellence. I amassed great wealth before opening a bank account or getting my first credit card because of the supportive environment that urged me to dream big from a very young age—my bold ambition and belief that it takes an entire community to propel an individual forward are some of my most treasured intangible assets.

And now as a wife and mother, I have a whole new mojo that comes from these newer roles in my life. There is no amount of money in the world that can give me the kind of wealth that my daughter, Gabrielle, who was born on April 26, 2019, can give me. My husband George and I struggled to conceive, and as I will share with you later, it was our faith that helped us to get through the dark days when we did not think we would be parents. Gabrielle represents the epitome of intangible wealth— she is a priceless asset that provides a lifelong return of joy. If you are a mother, you have intangible assets that go beyond the dollars that sit in your bank account, and thus you should measure your wealth along those intangible dimensions as well.

Say this boldly with me:

> *My wealth is made up of more than the dollars and cents that sit in my bank account.*

Wealth is about you having financial prosperity plus the peace of mind and personal power that come as a result of your intangible wealth. Moreover, I guarantee that your intangible wealth will unlock much tangible wealth in your life. If the COVID-19 pandemic has taught us anything around the globe, it's that holistic wealth matters. So, then, what do I mean by being a Wealthy Girl? I'm going to take you there now.

A Deeper Diver on the Wealthy Girl Journey

Being a Wealthy Girl is all about having a mindset rooted in the expansive definition of wealth that goes beyond what sits in your bank account. This kind of wealth is possible and guaranteed if you start and then consistently follow the steps that I outline in this book. It's not just my experience, but that of others who have become incredibly wealthy by doing the same things I'm sharing with you. But here's the thing: if you're not going to take action using what you learn in this book, it's not going to help you. This is a real journey with real steps.

Teaching a Wealthy Girl mindset is my rendition of the sassy girl, the one who's classy, who takes control and leads. And especially the one who doesn't leave so much on the table. I'll show you how to become that girl.

I want you to honor the "girl" in you, as defined by you. By the end of this book, you will understand that there is power in the unique way girls can create wealth for themselves and others. Being a "girl" is also a mind-state that harnesses the power of the collective. I want you to be that girl who has a community-centric mind to enable you to move forward a bit faster in achieving your wealth goals. My vision and hope for you are that you're not the only one who becomes a Wealthy Girl. Instead, you'll pay the Wealthy Girl mindset forward to friends and family, and your community. Additionally, you will come to understand that the path to becoming a Wealthy Girl is easier than you might currently think.

In this book I'm sharing insights from my years of learning and exposure from my Ivy League education and training within prestigious financial institutions. I am also sharing lessons learned from my own trial-and-error wealth-building practices outside traditional institutions. I'll share with you how to build your intangible assets, and pass them to the next generation. I will share with you what works and what doesn't, and save you the drama of making mistakes along the way.

I'll share with you all I've learned so that your journey to growing wealth will be easier and even fun. Finally note that becoming a Wealthy Girl is not about being greedy. Rather it's about owning your power, asking for what you want and choose, and then promising yourself and delivering on it. I'll show you how to take the steps that can make your life better, and how to be a role model for others that way.

Whether you're twenty-five or sixty-five, I *know* you, too, can get there. In other words, wealth accumulation is a very beautiful way to live your life, no matter how old you are. I know you can become a Wealthy Girl.

One last point before I get into it. If you identify as something other than a "girl," I welcome you. Whether you are cisgender male, gender nonconforming, transgender, or choose to identify yourself differently, I know that there is something in this book for you. If you do not personally pick up anything from the stories and advice that I share on the following pages, I have no doubt that there is someone in your life who can benefit from my words. In this sense, you can adopt the Wealthy Girl mindset and share the principles of this book with the girls whom you love. Us girls need your allyship and support along our journeys.

Now that you know a bit about my intention and background, I want to share the story of the Wealthy Girls who came before me. If you don't know that story, then you can't truly know much about me. If you don't know me, then it's hard to understand how I have become wealthy in the way I've defined it. These women are strong examples of Wealthy Girls, and understanding their full stories is critical to knowing what it takes to be a Wealthy Girl.

I was blessed enough to make it to thirty-eight with two grandmothers still living: Grandma Shine, my mom's mom, and Grandma Pearl, my dad's mom. Grandma Pearl died in 2018 at age ninety, and Grandma Shine turned ninety-two in 2020. Grandma Naomi Pinnacle Shine migrated from South Carolina to New York City in

1949, and Grandma Pearl Petite Conanan migrated from Alabama to New York City in the 1940s.

Both grandmas were two of the six million Blacks who fled the cruel, segregated South as part of the Great Migration from 1915 to 1970. Like the three Black migratory stories detailed in Isabel Wilkerson's *The Warmth of Other Suns*, they both left for a better life than what the Jim Crow South could offer. They wanted freedom. They tried to move away from the injustices and inequity that pressed down upon their necks in an oppressive, racist American South.

Sound familiar? We only have to dive into our recent memory in 2020 to relive the horrors of George Floyd, Breonna Taylor, Ahmaud Arbery, and Elijah McClain, and deeper in our history to honor the countless other Black bodies destroyed at the hand of oppression.

While my grandmas knew that they could not entirely flee American racism by moving from the South to the North, they had a better chance of staying alive, earning money, and making a good life for their future families. Grandma Shine made the train ride solo in her early twenties, while Grandma Pearl made the train ride with her sister as a teenager. Both grandmas had little luggage but limitless dreams for a better life. After settling in the North, my grandmas returned to the South only for funerals, reunions, and special birthdays.

Going back "down South" as they would say, often reminded them of a painful past that, on the one hand, they left behind, yet on the other hand, was their Black Southern roots that mainly influenced their New York City home through its loving familial bonds, community-driven support, and strong faith. They left behind a storied Southern history to build a wealthy life, defined on their own terms, in the North.

Grandma Shine and Grandma Pearl both settled in Harlem and married soon after their arrival in New York. They both had kids, and their eldest—Naomi's daughter Barbara and Pearl's son Frank—met each other in 1971, married in 1974, and then had children of their own. My brother Clayton was born in 1977, and I had the good fortune of popping out in 1980.

Though my Grandma Pearl was unable to work due to the onset of mental illness, she married Hermogenous Conanan, a Filipino immigrant whose job as chef in the U.S. Coast Guard provided enough wages for the two of them and their eventual three children to make it through the years. My grandparents eventually settled in the Italian, Filipino, and Puerto Rican immigrant-infused neighborhood of Cobble Hill, Brooklyn, in the late 1950s.

My grandparents bought a multiunit brownstone for $15,000 with money borrowed from one of my grandfather's brothers and quickly paid back that loan. Since then, there have been countless family gatherings, overflowing with my grandma's love, in that house over my forty years of life. My father and mother lived in the third-floor apartment for the first six years of their marriage, and I spent my first eighteen months living in that home. Although my grandmother and grandpa have passed away, their brownstone is now owned by my father and his siblings. They rent it out to tenants in what is now one of Brooklyn's poshest neighborhoods.

The house is worth many multiples above $15,000 today, and yet our memories are priceless. The house is one example of the tangible wealth created between generations. The love that has emanated from the people in that house is one example of the intangible wealth that I now have.

Now, my Grandma Shine began her working career in the North as a homemaker, at times making $2.50 per hour to help support a family of eight. While my grandfather Joseph worked the shipyards moving cargo, his paycheck wasn't enough to provide for their family of eight. It's important to know that Grandma Shine graduated valedictorian of her high school before making the trek North. But she was unable to earn a college degree because her family could not afford to send her to college. As such, though she highly valued formal education, working became her way up and out. And to her immense joy, all six of her kids went to college. The three girls went on to professional service careers. The boys found jobs with amazing pension benefits by working as a policeman, a correction officer, and a unionized trade artisan.

From 1950 to 1990, my Grandma Shine held down homemaker jobs, sometimes working two to three of them at a time. She would eventually move from "working for the man" at a homemaking company to her own independent contracting jobs, a sole proprietorship, in today's vernacular. Along the way, she cultivated a very strong network of other women, including relatives and friends who had also migrated from the South, to give them opportunities to work her jobs when she was oversubscribed. She thus provided other women with independent contracting opportunities to put more money in their pockets as well. She kept a lot of the dollars in her pocket by starting her business as an independent contractor, and although it was informal and she was far from monetarily rich, her income provided the necessary dollars and flexibility for her family to survive. The money accumulated from my Grandma Shine's sole proprietorship is one example of tangible wealth that helped her family survive. Grandma Shine's strong relationships with the women who came into her orbit and her value of education (formal and informal) are examples of the intangible wealth that has passed on to my mom and then to me.

I share my grandmas' stories because they both achieved varying degrees of financial prosperity over their lifetime and amassed a high degree of peace and personal power along the way. Their faithfulness in God is inspirational even to the most ardent atheists. Their journeys are the blueprint on which I have based my life and my own Wealthy Girl journey. My Wealthy Girl story will not end with me, but instead will pass on to my daughter,

Gabrielle, and if she is so fortunate to have a girl, on to her daughter.

I want to take you on a journey through these eleven chapters to help you bask in being a Wealthy Girl. I was where you are, sometimes doubting my abilities or failing to take action when I knew I should. Trust me, I found the way to pursue wealth, and so can you. I'll share my ups, downs, and everything around to find your path to wealth. But being a Wealthy Girl also means having freedom and opportunity in your life. Both of my grandmas possessed these intangible assets. Wealth is about fulfilling the desires you hold dearest to your heart. Isn't that the kind of wealth you want to pass down to your children, especially your daughters, who are born into a world that tries to box them in?

So I extend to you this invitation: Come, join me. Become a Wealthy Girl!

How to Use This Book

I will provide you with new ways of thinking about wealth using seven specific steps to help you achieve both tangible and intangible wealth, and detailed takeaways that summarize the main points for each chapter. In the takeaways, I will ask you several questions that I want you to ponder, and then leave you with a call to action. Yes, *action!* My hope is that you employ at least one of my strategies in your own life.

Don't worry. You are not alone. My deep desire is that through my words, you will feel me journeying with you in order to help you achieve your wildest, wealthy dream. Think of me as your accountability partner as you are reading. At the beginning of each chapter, I will openly and authentically share with you some of my own Wealthy Girl stories, as well as those of other women. I do this so that you can learn as many examples as possible from the journeys of others. You will read about the good, the bad, and everything in-between.

So, what are you really going to get out of this book? I'm going to give you insights in a way that's friendly, devoid of fluff, and practical, and one that more openly recognizes the structural forces that can often impede your individual wealth pursuits than you may have found in other books about finances. I break down complex concepts in an easy-to-understand manner. I'm opening the doors of wealth, as I've defined it. I'll be sharing with you all kinds of unique, action-oriented strategies that you might not have thought of before. For instance, I won't focus you on solely paying down debt, but rather on how you can execute on tangible investing strategies within traditional financial systems *and* build intangible Wealth Circles that subvert traditional financial systems. Both strategies will help change your life and build wealth holistically. From there you will learn the power of changing other people's lives by paying your wealth forward.

So let's get right into it.

The following is a summary of each chapter. This is a cheat sheet on what to expect. In the beginning chapters, you will shift your mindset of what it means to be wealthy and understand what may be stopping you from achieving the wealth status you deserve. Then in the remaining chapters, I'll provide you the seven steps to achieve your Wealthy Girl status.

Chapter 1: Taking a New Wealth Journey. You're reading this one right now. Here I have redefined what it means to be wealthy and what I wish to offer you. As you keep reading, I will share relevant stories from my background and why I wrote this book for you, a Wealthy Girl.

Chapter 2: 8 Myths Stopping You from Being Wealthy. In this chapter I first debunk eight myths that I believe hold us back from being the Wealthy Girls we are meant to be. For instance, one of the myths that you might tell yourself is, "I'm not worthy of wealth." Don't believe this. I will help you get these myths out of your psyche so that you can get toward action.

Chapter 3: Step 1, Build an Environment for Wealth Creation (Part A). In this first step, I'll show you how to build a robust environment for wealth creation. It starts with the relationships in your life. I will give you strategies to surround yourself with love, to practice ambition, and to develop those long-lasting female bonds. You will learn how to start your Wealthy Girl journey with the right environment.

Chapter 4: Step 1, Build an Environment for Wealth Creation (Part B). Since building an environment for wealth creation is so important, in this chapter I will show you how to create your personal A-Team. I will get real on how to unleash the power of your A-Team, which includes one or more of the following: a career coach, a financial advisor, a peer mentor circle, a sponsor, and a therapist.

Chapter 5: Step 2, Work Your Craft. In this chapter, I will show you what it means to focus on something so intently that you develop a skill set. By drawing inspiration from someone who excels at their craft, making a commitment to learning (both formally and informally), and perfecting your craft, you will develop your Wealthy Girl mojo. I will share specific personal disciplines, such as journaling and protecting your time, which will help you work your craft. Finally, you will learn how to overcome the setbacks that will surely come when you commit to working your craft.

Chapter 6: Step 3, Develop an Investor Mindset. I will share the story of the greatest investor I know and the secrets that have made her successful. You will learn how to become the CEO of your wealth, how to invest in your dreams first, and how to utilize my own proprietary tangible wealth-building strategy called SIPPin' & Livin' — saving, investing, protecting, and paying down, plus living your life. This strategy has generated thousands of dollars for me and many other women.

Chapter 7: Step 4, Run Wealthy Experiments. My biggest experiment resulted in my marriage! In this chapter, I will give you a blueprint to experiment in your life, and how you can build wealth by doing so not only for yourself, but also for the generations that come after you. You will learn how to apply the culture of experimentation to your personal and professional life.

Chapter 8: Step 5, Start a Business or Support the Entrepreneurs and Small Businesses around You. As a founder of my own company and an investor in small businesses, I know the wealth effect of simply being around small businesses. In this chapter, I will share why it is so important to support the entrepreneurs in your life, or start your own business. More importantly, I will share the tips to get started and develop the right mindset for the journey.

Chapter 9: Step 6, Build a Faith Muscle. In this c hapter, I will define what I mean by faith, and a faith muscle, one of the most valuable intangible wealth attributes you can develop. I will give you the tools to define faith on your own terms, garner the support you need, and get the power to move on in life, even in disappointment. I end this chapter by sharing one of my favorite faith-building songs to encourage you on your own journey.

Chapter 10: Step 7, Be a Girl. The last step in being a Wealthy Girl is to simply be a girl. I don't define a girl by the physical gender that you were born into, or the one you may have chosen post-birth. I will show you how to apply the very traits that make us powerful women in order to build your wealth. Whether it's building your own Wealth Circle or getting the men around you to support you, you have the unique opportunity to leverage one of your greatest assets—the girl in you!

Chapter 11: Enjoy Your Wealth—Prosperity, Peace, and Personal Power Lived Out. Now that you have the seven steps to create wealth, you should enjoy it. There should be *lots* of fun when wealth is at the center of your life. If not, what's the point? I will show you what it looks like to live out a life of wealth, thereby obtaining that prosperity, peace, and personal power you deserve. Trust me, it's a joyful experience.

Each chapter builds on the previous one, and thus this book is perfect for you if you want to read it one chapter after the next. However, if you like jumping around, I've designed it so you can do that too, because the chapters mutually reinforce each other. Some chapters might be more relevant for you at one time than another. Therefore, I suggest you keep the book as a trusty guide over time. For instance, you may want to come back to certain chapters that pertain to challenges or opportunities that arise in your life. The lessons in this book will help you even more when you're going through something and could use a bit of timeless advice.

I encourage you to take notes as you read through the chapters, and feel free to come back to the chapters that resonate with you the most. However, the best way to use this book is to form a Wealth Circle of two or more people. You might be asking, what's a Wealth Circle? As I mentioned in my summary of all the chapters, I will share more with you how to create your own in Chapter 10.

In short, a Wealth Circle is a community of likeminded people, even if it's only one person—a best friend, a spouse, or a family member—who is vested in your success and wealth. Your Wealth Circle will help you stick with the strategies I share here. I've witnessed the power of one's Wealthy Girl network again and again and I know it will serve you well.

If my ninety-year-old grandmothers taught me anything, it's that you're never too old to take a new journey. So I'm throwing down the gauntlet and challenging you to take your best self, move it forward, and don't stop. Embrace your Wealthy Girl status and claim your destiny.

Let's go!

2

8 Myths Stopping You from Becoming Wealthy

BEFORE WE GET INTO the steps in your Wealthy Girl journey, I want to share several common myths that might be blocking your path. Hopefully, these will help you, once and for all, break through to your road to success. I'm excited to share what I've learned from thousands of hours talking with (and helping) individuals with their wealth and money.

While the following eight myths are common, you may not have experienced every one of them but you likely know someone who believed in and followed many of them. Well, I want to bust these myths, not only to liberate you, but also to liberate the other girls in your life. The truths about these myths have empowered me in my life as a Wealthy Girl. I hope that the same happens to you.

Myth 1: Wealth Is Only What's in My Bank Account

I'm a math geek. I admit it. I believe in the power of numbers. However, the belief that your wealth is only defined by the money that sits in your bank account is a big myth. I want you to base your wealth not solely on your bank account, but also on your values and your intangible assets.

For instance, the gender pay gap, or the difference in earnings between women and men, is extremely wide. It makes sense then that if you earn less money as a woman, then your ability to save and invest or accumulate traditional wealth will be limited to some extent.

The Center for American Progress reported an analysis of 2018 Census Bureau data and found that "women of all races earned, on average, just 82 cents for every $1 earned by men of all races" in the U.S.[5] Despite various attempts to measure the gender pay gap, there is broad consensus in its conclusion: women consistently earn less than men, and the gap is wider for most women of color. Reasons cited for this gender pay gap are differences in industries or jobs worked, differences in years of experience, differences in hours worked, and discrimination. Specifically, discrimination is understood to account for more than 38 percent of the gender pay gap. In 2019, more than 55 million full-time working women collectively earned an estimated $546 billion less than their male counterparts. More disturbing is this: in the absence of updated and comprehensive equal pay reform, the gender wage gap has closed by only four cents in more than a decade. At that pace, women are not estimated to reach pay parity with men until 2059.[6] Lower earnings surely contribute to the accumulation of less wealth since you cannot make the choice to save or invest what you do not earn, and thus cannot grow your asset base as quickly.

Furthermore, there is a staggering racial disparity when it comes to traditional wealth in the U.S. I care about these statistics a lot as a Black woman, and if you're a woman of color across any diaspora, I'm sure you know these statistics very well. For example, as recently as 2016, a typical white family's net worth at $171,000 is almost ten times greater than that of a Black family at $17,150. The inequality of wealth between Black and white households unveils the aftermath of accumulated inequality, racism, and discrimination. Additionally, the out-of-balance discrepancies in opportunity and power stretch back to the very founding of this country. The wealth gap between Blacks and whites reveals a society that historically has not and still does not extend equality of opportunity to all its citizens.[7]

The harsh reality is that these statistics, both the gender pay gap and the racial wealth gap, are bleak and can deflate even the most ardent optimist. Who wants to wait another forty years before we fix the gender pay gap, and perhaps way longer to fix the racial wealth gap? Not me. Given all of the complex structural and systemic issues that contribute to these statistics, they can feel insurmountable and unachievable.

So, what can you do?

First, you should certainly acknowledge the incredible systemic forces at play, and these forces will always coexist with your individual efforts to gain tangible wealth. To fix these systemic issues, our country will need sweeping legislation, tax reform, and policies of traditional wealth redistribution.

In the interim, you should reframe your measurement of success. In *Ain't I a Woman: Black Women and Feminism,* bell hooks describes how America has been built on patriarchal values, and specifically white patriarchal values, and these measures of worth are inadequate given the colonial and imperialist value system that they are based in. Addressing feminist movements' attempts to advance women's rights, hooks urges women, especially Black women, to question the white patriarchal systems that never had them in mind in the first place.[8]

Similarly, why should we measure our wealth success solely by traditional measures since women, especially those of color, weren't set up to achieve wealth through traditional systems in the first place? In essence, the system is flawed and broken, and thus measuring all of your wealth by the same system that has tried to lock you out only sets you up for disappointment. The bleak statistics are not only depressing, but also position women and Black people with a deficit framing; they always remind me of what I lack relative to another group. And I am reminded of these statistics pretty much every day. It becomes easy to tell myself this about wealth: "Hey girl, the statistics are bleak, and I will never get ahead."

I agree with hooks's insistence in reframing how we define ourselves and our wealth. We are far more than tangible wealth data, and we should be measuring ourselves fully. It's time to define things on your own terms. This is not to assert that you should not look for ways to make progress along these traditional wealth measures, and increase your traditional wealth. In a later chapter I will show you how you can hack the existing system to obtain traditional wealth as well as create alternative, nontraditional avenues for obtaining tangible wealth.

I choose to look at the entire picture from an asset-framing perspective. Assets aren't just about the tangibility of how much money you have in the bank. Assets are intangible as well. So, when the statistics fall short of painting your full contributions or encapsulating the values that you care about, you must provide other descriptors of your wealth status. I want you to look at your contributions not by what you lack, but by what you add value toward. Consider asking questions such as "What other statistics capture my assets, both tangible and intangible? Or, "How do I want to define wealth for *my* life?"

Again, wealth is not only about the dollars and cents. While you may lack a tangible wealth perspective, you may be far ahead in terms of your intangible wealth. Here are some questions to ask:

- Do you contribute to your community with your time and talents?
- Do you pursue the cultural capital that we discussed in Chapter 1?
- Do you focus on the relationships around you, albeit with your family or friends?
- Do you believe in a higher power, or exercise an element of faith?

Your answers to these questions will help you get at the heart of your intangible wealth and should not be overlooked.

Men are often socialized to define themselves by their paychecks. On the other hand, as women, more often than not we don't define ourselves similarly. Instead, we look at more values-based factors, such as the communities that we touch, our ability to reproduce, our ability to partner up, and the list goes on and on.

Recognize that it's a myth that your wealth is only what's in your bank account. You are far more than what these numerical statistics would have you believe. So, start to expand your definition of wealth.

Myth 2: There Is Only a Select Group of Wealthy, White People

The second myth is that there is only a select group of wealthy, white people. This one is extremely far from the truth. I found out that traditional wealth (the dollars and cents of it) wasn't concentrated in just a few people's hands. This insight came during the time I started my college journey at Yale University. My intuition told me that many students, and their families, would have wealth. After all, it is an Ivy League school!

At first, looking at the faces of my many white class-mates in my Yale Facebook, the physical bound book—and the precursor to the digital Facebook we all know today— reinforced this myth. My thoughts went something like, "Wow! These are white people who come from families that are probably very wealthy." You see, I had ascribed wealth to whiteness and white people. When I got on campus, however, I met several Black people who I found out came from very traditional wealthy families. Now, these wealthy Black students were still grossly outnumbered by their white wealthy peers, but I was still fascinated that people who looked like me had parents who owned planes!

At the same time, I struggled with my own sense of belonging. Though I considered myself a confident person, I believed and feared that people would look at me and say to one another something like, "She only got into Yale because of affirmative action," notwithstanding the fact that I earned higher than a 4.0 GPA when factoring in my Advanced Placement classes, took seven Advanced Placement classes, graduated salutatorian from my high school of six hundred students, and had excelled in many extracurricular activities. If I didn't quite fully believe that

I belonged, how could I possibly believe that I could also obtain the wealth of my peers?

I didn't have the language to articulate why I felt like my achievements were not as good (or better) relative to my white peers when I was eighteen years old, but I know now that the forces of racism and internalized racial oppression were at play. It's important to take a step back to define both terms clearly so that we have a shared understanding of the forces that affect us *all*.

The antiracism training organization Crossroads, from which I've taken several courses, defines racism as "racial prejudice plus the misuse of power by a dominant group, enforced by the systems and institutions of a society, giving power and privilege based on race to the dominant group, and limiting the power of privilege of the racial groups that are not in power."[9] In America today, the dominant group are persons defined as *white* and the subjugated group are persons defined as *people of color*. I define myself as a person of color, and specifically Black with Filipino roots. And, internalized racism, in "Flipping the Script: White Privilege and Community Building" can be defined by these important facets:[10]

- **As people of color are victimized by racism, we internalize it**...just as there is a system in place that reinforces the power and expands the privilege of white people, there is a system in place that actively discourages and undermines the power of people and communities of color and mires us in our own oppression.

- **Because internalized racism is a *systemic oppression*, it must be distinguished from human wounds like self-hatred or "low self-esteem," to which all people are vulnerable.** It is important to understand it as systemic because that makes it clear that it is not a problem simply of individuals. It is structural. Thus, even people of color who have "high self-esteem" must wrestle with the internalized racism that infects us, our loved ones, our institutions, and our communities. Internalized racism must, then, be understood as a system to be grappled with.

- **Internalized racism negatively impacts people of color intra-culturally and cross-culturally.** Because race is a social and political construct that comes out of particular histories of domination and exploitation between peoples, the internalized racism of people of color often leads to great conflict among and between them as other concepts of power—such as ethnicity, culture, nationality and class—are collapsed in misunderstanding.

The important lesson here? Understand the systemic forces that can make you feel that tangible wealth is often reserved only for white people, when in fact wealth is available to nonwhite individuals. It takes constant work, even now, to recognize and attempt to act against internalized racial oppression because racism shows up in my life on a daily basis. Though a constant battle, it's worth it to continue to fight against these forces.

I eventually came to realize that I belonged at Yale. This revelation was enlightening because it helped me to understand that there's not a limit to the number or color of wealthy people, that I could have traditional wealth as well, and not all wealthy people are white.

You can shift your mindset toward gaining wealth by exposing yourself to others who look similar to you and who have had trajectories toward living a life that you define as wealthy, by the terms you see as important. For example, while reading Michelle Obama's book *Becoming*, I saw myself in her story. We both come from a background of strong family connections and a desire to excel at school. It hit me, "Yeah, look at Michelle. She is now amazingly wealthy. I can be that way, too." Actually believing that you can be wealthy helps you get to a place where you don't see wealthy people as a subset of the population that's exclusive and unattainable.

Another person who I looked to for confirmation that I too could become wealthy is Katherine Johnson, who has long been one of my sheroes. She passed away at the age of 101 early in 2020. Johnson, a woman of color, was a phenomenal mathematician. She worked at NASA's Flight Research Division for 33 years. NASA tried to prevent her from contributing to its objectives because of her gender and the color of her skin.[11] But she continued to persevere in a racist and sexist system. Eventually, her calculations created the precise trajectories that in 1969 paved the way for Apollo 11 to land on the moon, and following astronaut Neil Armstrong's historic first moonwalk, allowed the spacecraft to return to Earth.

Despite Johnson's incredible contributions to space and American history, few people had ever heard of her until Taraji P. Henson portrayed her in the 2016 multi-award-winning film *Hidden Figures*. Even though mass recognition of her achievements took decades, Johnson's skills and accomplishments will never be forgotten. Her stature, position of influence, and skillful contributions to NASA and American history—which are incredible intangible assets—made her, and all of us, wealthy. She defies the myth that wealth is reserved for white people, and thus reflects what I consider to be the epitome of the Wealthy Girl.

Who are other Wealthy Girls that you admire who look like you, and should serve as a reminder that wealth can look different than what society might have us believe? Have you taken stock of the systemic forces around you that might be influencing your approach to wealth?

Myth 3: I'm Not Worthy of Wealth

Women especially are often encumbered by a belief that they are not worthy of wealth. I've talked with hundreds of women about wealth over the years, and they will not make statements like the one above, outright in a group setting. But after digging deeper, I usually end up having an individual conversation where they will ask questions such as: "Can *I* really ask for that kind of raise from my employer?" or "Do you really think *I*, who live paycheck to paycheck, would be able to live any differently?"

At the root of these questions is the underlying belief, "I am undeserving of good things showing up in my life, either due to past experiences," or fear of their own greatness translating into wealth. In my own conversations and workshops, men don't seem to be saddled with this self-doubt.

Let me bring this myth home with an example from popular culture. In the movie *The Color Purple,* based on Alice Walker's book, which stars Whoopi Goldberg (Celie) and Margaret Avery (Shug), there is a scene where Celie is all dressed up in a beautiful costume of royalty. Here, Shug asks her directly, "Oh, Miss Celie. Why you always covering up your smile?" referring to Celie's tendency to constantly hide her smile by putting her hands over her mouth. Shug goes on to say, "You see Miss Celie, you have a beautiful smile."

At this moment, Shug affirms Celie's important existence and her beautiful smile. Until then, Celie had been conditioned to shrink into the background of life, which, though incredibly painful, she continued to do even when she was not in a painful circumstance. But Shug's recognition of her special and unique presence helps Celie realize that she deserves to show her smile and her whole self to the world. Shug shows Celie, also, she is worthy of attention.

There are many women who can relate to Celie's story and that dull, life-sapping normalcy of feeling unseen and unworthy, which translates into all facets of their lives, including their attainment of wealth.

But I'm here to tell you straight out:

You are worthy and deserving of wealth.

If you have breath in your lungs, you should know that you are beautifully and wonderfully made, and your uniqueness is a key driver of your wealth.

As such, I dare you to make an investment in yourself, which is an investment in your future self and your future wealth. I'll explain this in greater detail in the pages that follow.

Myth 4: I Don't Have the Skill Set to Build Wealth

You might be plagued by a belief that you don't have a particular skill set that you need to acquire the kind of wealth you desire. This is a myth rooted in a mindset of personal lack, past mistakes, and a lack of confidence. Here you may tell yourself something like "Well, I didn't learn it when I was a kid, and I'm just bad with money," or "My husband is the one that handles the money for our household, and he's the one that's good with math and our finances."

Then often, you might absolve yourself from being informed about wealth strategies, or slip into unhealthy familiar patterns that keep you stagnant. Or perhaps you let someone else dictate what you should be doing with your money. You sway on a spectrum from self-pity to apathy, and then back again. Slowly, the belief that you don't really have what it takes to build wealth takes over your aura and prevents you from assuming your Wealthy Girl mojo.

What's even more alarming is that studies have shown that women, even when they are overqualified and over-prepared, hold back in the pursuit of the things they want, such as a job. For example, a study a few years ago by Hewlett Packard showed that women applied for a promotion only when they met 100 percent of the qualifications. Men applied when they met 50 percent.[12] Since women generally feel confident only when they are perfect or practically perfect, they are more susceptible to not taking action when it comes to obtaining their wealth goals. I will show you how to take action and build your confidence.

Your past experiences also may give rise to a fear that you will make the same mistakes going forward. That's a very human experience. I've been there. However, I know that you cannot stay in a state of fear because it will immobilize you. Don't worry. I'll show you how to build a faith muscle that will fight fear at its core. Use my mantra, "faith over fear," and you can have this message pervade your life too as it has helped me in my life.

Embrace the mindset that you are the CEO of your wealth. We will talk more about this in Chapter 6, but for now, when I say you are the CEO of your wealth I mean that you create the vision for how you want to build wealth, and what kind of life you want to have. After you establish your vision, it will become more of a process by which you can develop the Wealthy Girl skill set, and ultimately, educate yourself and build confidence, which will be key to your success. But being CEO of your wealth won't work if you do not believe that you are worthy to be that CEO (check back on Myth 3 if this is the case for you).

Now, it won't all come at the same time and you don't have to personally acquire every single skill set. Like all great CEOs, you will surround yourself with good advisors. These mentors will provide the support and complementary skills that will help you achieve your vision.

What I mean here is that you don't have to have all the toolkits and skill sets contained in *your* body and mind. You can create a great support team of people who specialize in the areas that are not your specialty. That's one of the reasons why I'm writing this book—I'm fortunate to be bolstered in the Wealthy Girl creation process by a great support system.

You can rely on the expertise of others, but you have to take the initiative to build your wealth and surround yourself with the people and the belief that you're not limited just because you didn't learn that from your mother or your father. And even if your partner handles the finances in your household today, you still owe it to yourself (and your household) to educate yourself and acquire a base level of knowledge so you can make the right decisions. The whole point is that wealth isn't rocket science. Once you have the belief that you can obtain it, actually it's quite simple. Keep reading—I'm going to show you how.

Myth 5: Wealth Is Acquired Not by Hard Work, but by Luck or Inheritance

Many people still believe that wealth is not acquired through skill or hard work, but rather that it occurs due to luck or inheritance. Others still subscribe to the belief that people who are wealthy are born that way, with the proverbial silver spoon in their mouth. They start out in the world from their lofty tower of wealth and affluence. That does happen sometimes, but it surely isn't the case all the time.

There's also a prevailing belief that goes something like this: "Oh, this person just knew that person," and was somehow magically in the right place at the right time to begin growing their traditional wealth. Don't get me wrong, sometimes people *are* simply lucky, and shoot! I think anyone would take luck. I want to point out, however, it's not just knowing people, but it's *how* they know you.

If you build value-based relationships, your destiny becomes, "It's not just who you know, it's *how* you know them and *what value* is exchanged between the two of you." I'm not talking about money value as much as about what my publisher and author of one of the best-selling books (ranked at #10 for a year on Amazon) on networking called *Networlding*, Melissa G. Wilson, calls "The Great Exchange."

Here, values-driven networkers help one another through ongoing *exchanges* of support that move from the starting level of emotional support to information on up through wisdom, leads, referrals, and ultimately co-creative support to our respective communities. Melissa and I were connected by a common friend, and I chose Melissa as my publisher because of our own values-driven exchange.

What Melissa's research and support to individuals, entrepreneurs, and corporations has proven over the last fifteen years is that people who build vibrant networks of supporters with like values can leverage their networks to achieve great wealth. But even more than that, Melissa would add, the Networlding system helps those who care deeply about values like integrity, making a difference, and collaboration, realize that one can not only achieve a wealthy life, but a life of service and constant support and . . . even fun! A lot of wealthy people work very hard. It may sometimes seem like they don't, but that's because many of them have been working at their craft for a very long time (or have been exposed to someone else who has acquired wealth), so it appears to people on the outside that their wealth journey comes with no work at all. In reality, however, many wealthy people have put in many hours to maintain and grow their wealth, or have spent a lot of hours soaking up the experience of others who are wealthy, regardless of how they got it. For instance, I think about Sonja Gamby, who happens to be my cousin and godsister.

Sonja expects to receive her doctorate in chemistry education at the University of New Hampshire in 2021. She is an assistant professor at North Shore Community College in Massachusetts. She has made it her professional and personal mission to ensure that her students know the ins and outs of chemistry. When I visited Sonja's chemistry lab back in 2010 as she pursued her master of science degree at the University of Maryland College Park, I remember how hard she worked at growing bacteria cultures and conducting chemistry experiments. Her diligence was admirable, especially since I had absolutely no clue what she was doing. While I loved science, I realized that Sonja's chemistry pursuits were next level. It was clear that she had spent hours learning and working on her chemistry craft. And she did so during that period while mothering her first child.

Her work ethic came shining through again in 2019 when I read her research proposal for her dissertation paper, entitled "Development and Characterization of Contextualized Metacognitive Interventions that can be Integrated into Chemistry Courses." I know, doesn't the title alone sound like she put a lot of hours into the paper? That's because she did. This time, Sonja did so while raising three kids and trying to attend their many activities, including swim meets, tennis matches, karate practices, and piano lessons, just to name a few. She is the definition of a Wealthy Girl.

Soon, we'll talk more about working your craft and creating an environment built on relationships that breed wealth. For now, know that wealth is not always the result of luck or inheritance.

Myth 6: Wealth Comes from Taking Big Risks, and I'm Risk Averse

When it comes to this myth, I've discovered that people sometimes adopt a mindset that they have to swing big, betting the farm, in the hope of acquiring wealth. In other words, if you're not of that mindset to "go big or go home" because you might be risk-averse, then, *darn it!* You missed out on the opportunity to get wealth and be wealthy!

But the reality is that every day, our lives are affected by the many small decisions that we make. Whether it's connecting with a friend or supporting someone at work, life can become so much more fulfilling when you focus on your *personal impact.* Ask questions such as, "What can I do today to share my impact with the world?" "How are all my activities that I'm doing lining up with the person that I want to be?" or "Today, where can I shine my light?" Satisfaction blossoms inside of us through our small daily habits aggregated together. These small but impactful moments create a wealthy life. You must remove misconceptions that your life is defined by big moments and tangible opportunities.

Remember the definition of wealth I presented earlier—it involves both the tangible and intangible aspects of having the life you want.

You don't have to exercise fear about the way you're going to live your daily life. I want to encourage you to do this instead: if you consider yourself a risk-averse person, breaking down your personal dreams and desires into bite-sized pieces can greatly help you build the kind of wealthy life that you want. Don't frame your mission around wealth building in terms like, "Oh, I'm not comfortable taking risks." Risk is very subjective.

Wealth comes from making daily commitments and having those commitments intentionally build a life that, when you look back on it, feels satisfying. You can breathe easy and feel great because you know, "I gave it my all today." That's a Wealthy Girl!

Myth 7: Wealth Can Only Be Acquired at the Expense of Others

I don't want to make this book about politics, but I offer this for your consideration because many people today believe that we had a real example in 2020 of someone who has gotten wealthy at the expense of pretty much everybody. If you haven't figured it out yet, I'm talking about 45. You have heard of this person.

He was elected to the presidency of the United States of America in a manner that shamefully affirmed everything that he has stood for, including cheating people, stepping on people's throats, and being narcissistic, racist, and misogynistic, just to name a few. He somehow landed himself in the White House.

So when we look at the forty-fifth president of the United States, it's a given that most of us are going to believe that wealth can be acquired at the expense of others, because the very person who led the U.S. for four years obtained his wealth, status, and power in this way.

That can then become a model for people to look at and say with a side-eye, "Hmm." As much as you might disagree with how he obtained his wealth, the reality is that he still became POTUS and we voted him in. A natural conclusion might be that wealth can only be acquired at the expense of others because the forty-fifth president, the one who led the most powerful country in the world, represented us in a very real way.

Perhaps you think this might not be the best example, but for me, it's such an egregious example that we must consider it representative of how some people really perpetuate their wealth. Some people in the U.S. who are tangibly wealthy, which affords them a position of power, have in fact gained that wealth and power at the expense of others. But I also believe that this is the exception rather than the rule. The forty-fifth POTUS surely does not embody my standard of wealth when I define wealth expansively.

Unfortunately, we often do not talk about the wealthy people who treat people nicely and do not take advantage of others. Those people are not as appealing to the media, and the masses. There are lots of people who don't have that platform or agenda. They're just doing their thing and living their life. You can find plenty of stories about people who have gotten wealthy by improving and enhancing the community that surrounds them. You just have to redefine what "wealthy" entails as we have talked about. Look for it around you every day.

While writing this book during the 2020 COVID-19 pandemic and resulting quarantine, I reflected on my relationships with women in positions of power who not only helped push me forward, but did so with grace along the entire way.

One of these relationships started after I decided to attend the University of Chicago Booth School of Business (which you will read more about in Chapter 7, where I talk about running wealthy experiments). I chose Booth, in part, due to my interest in their reputable venture capital and entrepreneurship program. Given my initial desire to transition into the venture capital world after business school, Booth provided fertile ground to make that leap. I sought advice from current students about how to take advantage of the two-year Booth program, and one student encouraged me to actively reach out to two or three venture capitalists *before* arriving on campus in order to surround myself with industry experts who could potentially advise me throughout my business school journey.

It was great advice. There was one problem though: I didn't know any venture capitalists. So I did what was necessary. I researched venture capitalists in New York City whom I could draw out *any* connection with and sent them a cold email (I found their emails with the help of Google). I shared more about me, including my pending path to business school, and acknowledged how inspired I was when reading about their journey.

Out of the five people I emailed, one returned my note. Her office was located in Midtown Manhattan, just a few blocks away from where I was working at J. P. Morgan. Her picture on the venture firm's website expressed confidence and warmth, in addition to power; it evoked "I'm a boss and I've made money." She had a very accomplished bio, including her position as the co-founder of the venture firm StarVest Partners. Under her picture read the name Jeanne M. Sullivan.

Jeanne did not have to return my email, but I am so grateful that she did. She told me that she wanted to push other females forward in the field. Jeanne's return of my email became the start of a wonderful relationship. When I decided not to pursue the venture capital route in favor of starting my own business, Jeanne became an official advisor to my company, Smarteys. She opened doors for me that I would not have been able to open by myself, made numerous connections for me during my entrepreneurial journey, provided sound advice to the company, and made the time to meet for a cup of tea or lunch whenever I made it back home to New York City.

Jeanne officially became my mentor, and then sponsor (and we'll talk about the difference in Chapter 4), and eventually, my friend. I made important connections for her too, and we formed a mutual respect for who we were as people. When I told her that the journeys of white women and Black women in their pursuit to build tech companies and raise venture funding are incredibly different, she listened and acknowledged her own white privilege.

I will never forget the large bouquet of flowers that I found on my doorstep one Thanksgiving morning after I had a rough week. While we do not talk as often as we would like to today, she was so present during a special season in my life. Jeanne is a Wealthy Girl.

I believe some of us have a perception that people are wealthy because of actions that they have taken that put other people down, that aren't fair, and that they take advantage of situations.

Not all wealthy people treat others unfairly, or gain wealth at the expense of others. I don't want you to believe this myth. Many wealthy people, like Jeanne, treat others fairly and have a degree of generosity. You too have the opportunity to treat people nicely and fairly as you build and maintain your wealth. You can be that Wealthy Girl!

Myth 8: Wealth Is a Result of One's Individual Achievements

The last important myth that might plague you is that wealth is a result of individual achievement. The myth of individual achievement is rooted in Western ideals of individualism, which rewards and celebrates individual effort. This can be said of much of Europe and the U.S., as a rule.

Where I believe non-Western countries get it right is that they acknowledge the community over the individual.[13] African and Asian cultures are among those that tend to focus more on a collectivist/community ideal, as opposed to individualistic cultures where people generally perceive themselves as being defined by their personal traits and achievements and consider themselves separate from others. People in non-Western cultures are also more likely to consider themselves to be connected to others, and their sense of self is generally based on who they are when interacting with others, or by membership in a group.

Let's apply the concept of collectivism, or interdependence, to your wealth journey. Wealth is not obtained by individual achievement. Rather wealth is obtained when members of a community collectively help push each other forward. You are part of a larger community, and by being wealthy, you advance the wealth of others. Behind every wealthy individual, there's a whole team of people that helped them accomplish what they desire. The problem is that, more often than not, you don't see these people out front, and the result is damaging to our psyches: you develop a false perception of what it takes for an individual to become wealthy.

Mark Zuckerberg, the CEO of Facebook, is the poster child for this myth. One need look no further than the movie *The Social Network* to get a glimpse of how Zuckerberg's achievements are the result of the community— fellow developers, venture capitalists, his partner—that made an active decision to propel him forward. Yes, he worked hard! But there were many people who rallied behind (and with) him in order for him to achieve his success.

The myth of individual achievement is also troubling because it causes you to doubt yourself in some mighty ways, especially as you compare your wealth status to others without knowing their complete story. I call this the *comparisonitis* syndrome. You will probably ask yourself some version of this question: "What am I doing wrong, and why does this other person [fill in the blank] have what I want, even though it seems like I'm working hard as well?"

I had these same doubts and questions when I started my business and found myself comparing my journey to others' without fully understanding their full picture. I'll talk more about my experience in Chapter 8.

For now, stop comparing yourself to others. Your wealth journey is uniquely your own. Period. You sometimes *do not* know the community that stands around other people that helps them achieve their wealth. When you *do* know the community around them, ask yourself, "What elements of their community can I model for myself in a way that can help propel me forward in my unique way?"

The community of people that surrounds you is critical to your wealth. Remember, it does indeed take a village not only to raise a child, but also to become wealthy overall. And once you are wealthy, you have a responsibility to advance the wealth of others because you're pouring back into the community. The pay-it-forward mentality is quintessential to being a Wealthy Girl. Are you ready?

Chapter Takeaways

Now that you have gone through the myths that may well have previously stopped you from advancing toward a wealthy life, I ask you:

Which myth(s) resonate with you the most?

You might want to think about this question for a while, and you should take the time you need because you might have to dig deep and be honest with yourself.

Once you've identified the myth(s), share your myth(s) with someone in your life that you trust (and perhaps someone in your Wealthy Girl circle). Then ask this person if they would do you the honor of checking in with you six months from now to find out whether you are busting that myth apart. Accountability helps—again, you are a product of your community.

Everyone has their own unique perspective on money and their relationship to it. You'll learn a lot about mine as we journey through this book together. I invite you to spend some time thinking about your own relationship with money before going any further, perhaps to even journal a bit about it. And, since wealth is way beyond just money, I challenge you to expand your perspective on wealth.

Let me repeat: being wealthy is different from being rich! Wealth is about the tangible and intangible assets that give you the freedom and opportunity to live the life you desire. Write down all of your wealth attributes. And, by the time you finish reading this book, I am confident that you will add to the list. It will be powerful to come back to your journal and see how your thinking may evolve by the end of the book.

The most important takeaway from this chapter is to identify the myths that may have blocked you from moving forward on your journey to becoming a Wealthy Girl.

It is time to share the steps that will help you overcome these myths, and become a Wealthy Girl.

Let's roll.

3

Step 1: Build an Environment for Wealth Creation (Part A)

B UILDING A ROBUST ENVIRONMENT for wealth creation should be a key goal in your Wealthy Girl journey. Of course, some are just fortunate to be born into a family where a wealthy mindset is nurtured from birth. But the majority of us must take the lead to shift our mindsets and habits in ways that help us build that all-important wealthy environment. To help you move forward on your wealth-creation path, I'll begin by sharing a story from my years in sports, and then add a second example of the two most famous sibling tennis champs the world has ever known. Right up front, I'll tell you that I'm no tennis phenom.

In fact, I actually felt the sport was quite boring when I was growing up. Even so, I decided to try out for the varsity tennis team as a senior in high school for one reason, and one reason only. You see, I had set a big goal for myself:

to win the prestigious Scholar Athlete Award, which was bestowed upon the senior graduate with the most varsity letters in high school combined with the highest unweighted GPA.

I knew that if I could get a fall varsity letter, it would put me in the running, at least on the sports side. And since I'd always earned good grades, I knew the academic side of things would work itself out. So, the only fall sport that offered me a decent shot at making the varsity team was tennis. I already knew the winter and spring seasons would be filled by varsity basketball and varsity track contenders, respectively, since I had been playing on those varsity teams since I was a freshman in high school.

Thankfully, I made the varsity tennis team at the beginning of the fall season. I even received the title of "Most Improved Player." (The irony of that honor is that I literally had the most room to improve, since the majority of my teammates were so much better than I was. I still took the honor and ran with it!) My thought at this time was along the lines of, "If not now then when would I go all out to move forward and prove not only to my family but to others that I could try something new and succeed?"

But there is no question that my claim to fame in playing tennis was almost all due to Michelle, my best friend in high school. Michelle was a natural. She had also played tennis throughout her young life. And thankfully, we were set to play doubles tennis together. The only true regret I have about our doubles experience is that I accidentally hit her in the face with a racket during one of our tennis matches. As a result of my mistake, my dear friend has a scar on her nose to this day.

But back to the story. During our senior year, Michelle and I just vibed. We were already the best of friends, a relationship that started as neighbors when we were eight years old. We grew up literally right around the corner from each other. But once I joined the tennis team when we were seventeen, our friendship expanded to a whole new level. She's also the person who introduced me to sisters Venus and Serena Williams back in 1997, when they were just starting to become known.

Born in 1980, Venus is my age, while Serena is two years behind her. So 1997 was when I really started to pay attention to them as both a tennis duo and as sisters. I loved watching their lives unfold in the public eye. Fast forward: I'm now 40 years old, and Venus and Serena Williams are still playing tennis and rocking the world with their talent.

What I gleaned most, though, from watching them over the years is that there would be no Venus or Serena without their father. I think many people are aware of the way in which Richard Williams taught them from a very young age how to play the game. But more importantly, he taught them to stay *inspired* to *aspire* to greatness. They grew up in a nurturing family environment of trust. Their father and coach consistently reinforced in them the belief that they could be number one at any and all tennis championships. His philosophy, "Nothing is difficult unless you allow it to be. If you feel that people cannot stop you, that attitude radiates like heat on a highway,"[14] was one that both of his daughters obviously took to heart.

I am also very aware of their mother's staunch support of them and their careers, because the camera has always tended to find its way to her during their games. As you watch their mom, you can tell just by the sheer nature of her presence that she is always in their corner.

So when I think about environments that have made them successful, that consistent presence plays a major factor. Obviously, we don't know what happens behind the scenes, but what I can glean is that support and consistent presence for their daughters from both parents. It was important and instrumental to the wealthy environment in which they grew up that they could blossom and aim for greatness.

Now, Serena clearly has earned the accolades of a number one sports-rated phenom. Still, it's hard to think about Serena without Venus, because the truth is, there would be no Serena without Venus. In Serena's own words, without her, she would not have the competitive spirit that she cultivated. When I think about wealth and wealth creation, I believe it's that love that emanates from such key relationships that builds the kinds of environments that bring out the best in people.

Who Is Going to Build You Up, in Love?

So when you think about wealthy environments, who are the people who are going to build you up, especially in love? Who are the people who are going to teach and mold? Who are the people who are going to play that support role and be physically and emotionally present for you? They might not be in the direct line of fire in practice like Mr. Williams was for his girls. But they may be consistently there for you, as Serena and Venus's mom has been present for them. Or maybe they have been there to push you to greater success, as the Williams sisters have always done for each other.

As for my personal family support story, my dad always came to my tennis matches. My mom was usually working during that time of the day. I want to share with you a bit of background about my wonderful parents. We'll come back to the fact that these two—Frank and Barbara— are literally my crush couple. They fell in love in college, committed themselves to each other and to careers where they both help people, had two kids, and moved to the suburbs. Each is incredibly special individually, but they are awesome as a couple. They are that couple! When I was less than two years old and my brother was four, we moved to Long Island. My dad had received his master's degree in recreational administration.

But he purposefully decided to switch careers in the early 1980s when my parents realized that if both of them had work schedules that extended into the evening, they couldn't be there to support their kids after school the way they truly wanted. So they made a joint decision to create an environment for their children where at least one of them could be there between the hours of three and six p.m., which was when we'd usually get home from school.

At that time, my dad began working on his second master's, in special education. This enabled him to make a career pivot and become a special education (or "Special Ed") teacher. So in essence, he had a fairly identical schedule to my brother and me, since he was home with us after three p.m. because he didn't have to work with students anymore. That's why when I was in high school, my dad was around for all of my sporting events. My dad truly loves sports, so his steadfast presence in cheering from the stands after school was a major way he supported me. From his encouraging chants, you would think *he* was trying to win the match.

And it was my mom's emotional presence that would complement my dad's physical presence. When I would get down on myself before I had tried out for the tennis team and I'd bemoan something along the lines of, "Well, I never played tennis, and I'm not even sure I'm going to make the varsity team as a senior," my mom was the one who gently got into my head with some simple but powerful reinforcement like, "Yeah, you can do it. It'll be fine."

She also helped remind me of my ultimate goal. "Charisse, tell me again why you decided to play tennis in the first place? Wasn't it because you are going to aim for that award that you wanted: being number one in your class at both sports and academics?" So that really did drive me to want to play, and I just constantly had them both in my mind and in my ear, reminding me to stay focused on the goal, and doing it in love.

Sadly, it's a cold hard fact that not every child is told that they have unlimited opportunities or comes from a household of love. Or, as an adult, you might have forgotten what a loving environment looks like in your life.

Enter ambition.

Practicing Ambition Is Necessary for a Wealthy Environment

At the core of ambition is an earnest desire for some type of achievement with intention, such as power, honor, fame, or wealth. It also holds within its core meaning the willingness to strive for attainment. Here, almost anyone can build their ambition muscles. But you do need to be ready to work hard and take action to realize the fruits of that hard work. While ambition is no substitute for love, an ambitious approach to life will create a love for self. And, if you do not love yourself first, no one will.

Whether you're a child or you have a child, there's nothing wrong with ambition. Maybe you don't have kids of your own, but you are in contact with other people's kids. Helping children to foster ambition is something that you can breathe into those young souls as you breathe it into yourself.

So can you take advantage of an ambitious approach to life? Shellye Archambeau seems to think it's possible. Archambeau is the author of an intriguing book titled *Unapologetically Ambitious*. She is one of Silicon Valley's premier Black female CEOs. Her story is inspiring and I mention it because so many children grow up with an emphasis on what they don't have, or are not told that they have unlimited opportunities. They are not given the freedom to explore their full potential nor the freedom to speak truth to the things that matter to them. In her book, Archambeau speaks truth to power-sharing with her readers on how to develop an ambitious spirit to achieve one's dreams.

In her book, Archambeau points out that ambition involves intentionality. She states, "Be intentional about everything you do, especially when it comes to your career. You own your career, you drive. Make sure people know what you want and what you're striving for. If the universe doesn't know what you want, the universe can't help you."[15] I agree with that advice because it puts the power in your hands to share what it is that you want in life.

Many of us are told that we might not be able to do X, Y, or Z because of where we come from and what we grew up having or not having. That harkens back to the myth, "I Don't Have the Skill Set to Build Wealth," I shared in Chapter 2, where you may believe that your past dictates your future and you cannot foster an ambitious spirit. No, no, no. You are capable of unleashing the ambitious power that every single individual is capable of owning. Every single person has a God-given uniqueness about them that allows them to find that ambition in their own way, and find that spirit of power in themselves.

When I was growing up, my mom would frequently tell me and my brother, "Ambition is a good thing," and the old adage, "Practice makes perfect." I know that some kids today might still hear those things. What I learned from this was the simple idea that by practicing you strive for improvement. And even though I know that I'm not perfect, my actions can strive toward perfection. Similarly, if you practice ambition, you'll move toward an ambitious nature and develop an attitude that you can do anything that you put your mind toward.

Practicing ambition also means surrounding yourself with people who have similar goals, or investing in an ambitious environment for your children. I always wanted to be the best in school because I had that spirit of ambition. And I wanted to be the best in art, too. Around the age of ten, I decided that I wanted to be an artist when I grew up. I'll share that story with you here because it's also about fostering connections with others in order to nurture your ambitious spirit.

One day my mom was talking to her friend Marilyn about my interest in art. Marilyn said, "Oh, our mutual friend Nanette's son, Michael, is going to this art class taught by this woman who only takes about ten or eleven kids a year." Shortly after their conversation ended, my mom called Nanette. Even though she was a mutual friend of hers and Marilyn, my mom had no idea that Nanette's son was taking art lessons. But through the power of connection, there my mom was, reaching out on my behalf. She told Nanette, "Hey, Charisse is really into art these days. Can you give me the name of the woman who teaches your son?"

When she heard how much the art classes cost, it was way more than my mom wanted to spend. But she chalked it up as an investment in me, and from the age of about ten or so, I ended up taking art classes with Mrs. Almer. When I talk about the environment of children's upbringing, education is not just about formal education. It's also about the experiences that you also have outside the "traditional realms."

For me, becoming a student in this art class created an environment where I was encouraged to explore my creativity. Until that time, I had been creating puzzles for hours or drawing on paper, and this weekly class really helped me explore and expand on that. I eventually ended up creating some really beautiful pieces that my mom and dad proudly hung up in our house.

To this day, they still have some of my artwork on display. I loved working in a variety of mediums from drawing to painting, pastels, and charcoal. When people came to the house, they would almost always ask if these paintings were professionally done. At the bottom right, there's my signature, and the year I completed each piece. We each got to pick out what we wanted to draw and it wasn't the same thing every week. I loved the individual attention I received, as well as all of the other kids, because everyone was working on their own version of Picasso. It was very gratifying because I could work hard and take my time and Mrs. Almer would provide pointers and feedback to push my artwork to a new level.

I also received important validation from Mrs. Almer, who told me that I could be an artist if I wanted to pursue art professionally. I actually believed Mrs. Almer. Her words bred confidence in me as she spoke truth into my dreams. She's an outstanding example of someone else who might not be in your circle in the beginning but can very well evolve into a significant support person and influence. Her presence contributed greatly to my personal wealthy environment. While I never became a professional artist, my desires to confidently exercise my creativity through photography, take art classes from time to time, and use the right side of my brain—even in writing this book—are directly the result of my childhood art journey.

My art experience and the positive reinforcement I received also spilled over into confidence in playing sports, confidence in how I looked at myself overall. My family always told me that I was beautiful. So I didn't lack that kind of validation in the home environment. But when I was away from home and out in the world, art was something in which I could excel, and that gave me the confidence to take into other areas of my life. I might not have been the best in every single thing I tried. I knew that I wasn't the best basketball player or the best track star. But I believed that I belonged, and I made varsity in track, and varsity basketball as a freshman. All of that sprang from the confidence that I felt like I could reach certain levels.

Your ambitious pursuits will breed confidence in your capabilities—an intangible asset that begets wealth. You have the opportunity to channel that confidence in all aspects of your life, thereby generating the wealthy life you so deserve. And what better way to practice ambition than with other Wealthy Girls in your life?

Building Lasting Female Bonds Is Irreplaceable

The quote, "You're the average of the five people you spend the most time with," is often attributed to motivational speaker Jim Rohn. While you may not totally subscribe to that theory, I'm here to encourage you to ask yourself to look at this close group of five or more people and really identify where they fit in your life. Who are they? Family, friends, teachers, colleagues, etc. After you've done that, see if you can answer this question: "When needed, are these people there for me more than half of the time?"

As I mentioned earlier in this chapter, when I joined the tennis team during my senior year in high school, my friendship with my friend Michelle blossomed to a new level. She had such a pure love for the game, she inspired me to really give it my best effort. Being able to draw from somebody else's love for something can be doubly inspiring because it also gives you a peek at what drives them. Whenever someone is moved to dedicate their time to mastering something, it sets off an aha moment within you and you begin thinking along the lines of, "Well, what could I achieve if I dedicated my time to this?" Your original intention for taking up a new sport, hobby, or skill might be different than theirs, but you're able to customize it and make it your own.

To this day, Michelle is still one of my best friends, and more like a sister than a friend. She has been present for all seasons of my life, supporting me, sharpening me, pushing me, praying for me, and caring about me through the ups and downs. She is the kind of person with a heart of gold who anyone would be blessed to call a friend. Michelle is my "ride or die" sister who would literally go to the ends of the earth and back if I asked her. Michelle is emblematic of those special people who can assist us in so many ways, such as removing a lot of undue pressure, even pressure that you might be putting on yourself. And when we develop close bonds with amazing individuals in that category, we simply want to be aware of reciprocating the favor anytime we have the chance.

Perhaps you're at a juncture in your life where you're trying to figure out how to form lasting bonds with people, especially in a social media culture where strong bonds can feel out of reach, and you can feel more disconnected than ever given the multitude of surface-level interactions.

And, to top it off, adult friendships can be tougher to establish and maintain. You may be wondering, "How do I find them?" Wherever you are on your journey and whoever is in your inner circle, please bear in mind an old axiom: "You're a product of your environment." So, reviewing your list of close friends, are they contributing to your life in a very positive, wealth enhancing way? And if they aren't, where do you start looking?

I'd like to suggest first of all that you imprint that desire into your consciousness as a goal. Then begin to speak life to that. Share it with your remaining inner circle of people in your life just as you would when seeking a job. Something such as, "Hey, I'm looking for some new supportive friends because I value my own time, and I value people who want to put time and effort into me. People that I can give back to as well, as you and I do." This is something I tell my close friends a lot, as well as my husband. "We have to have equal reciprocity in our relationship." So your first step is to speak life to that.

Next, I would journal about it. Putting things down on paper helps us make our goals more tangible and real. Then personally, I would pray about it. If you're a believer in the power of prayer, it really can open you up to more positive possibilities in life. Then I might mention to others whom I consider more as acquaintances at the moment than close friends, "You know what? I'm looking for some more good girlfriends that really can support me and I can support." I have often found it incredibly interesting how the universe tends to open up possibilities and even miracles just by speaking life into your goals.

For me, lasting bonds with females have come in various forms; some, like my relationship with Michelle, have been around since childhood, while others, like my relationship with Bethany, have formed in new environments or transitions, and still others, like my relationship with Ayanna (who you'll hear more about in a minute), have emerged at certain life stages.

All of them have been orchestrated by God—there's no other way to explain the uniqueness and depth of each of them. I've learned that making the commitment to value (and thus put time into) these female relationships has the potential to generate so much wealth in life. I want you to experience that kind of wealth as well. As you think about your own female bonds or your desire to form new ones, reflect on your own season in life, and whether or not you are creating space for these relationships to flourish in your own life.

Sometimes getting started is the hardest part. So, in addition to providing a glimpse of how Michelle and I deepened our bond, I'll share the origin stories of my bonds with my friends Bethany and Ayanna.

On the first day that I arrived on Yale's campus to begin my freshman year, I met Bethany. We were assigned as roommates, which speaks to how lucky I got. When we first met, I had no idea that we'd be as close as we are today because there were so many differences on the surface. She was from Arizona, and I was from New York. She wore bright colors all the time, and I wore blacks and browns. She preferred reading a book to going out to a party, and I preferred going out dancing to reading a book for leisure.

And, yet by November of our freshman year, we knew we were going to be friends for life. We were so right. We were roommates all through college and then continued as roommates in Brooklyn, New York, for three years after college. When I talk about someone who I share my inner-most fears and doubts with, who shows up for me in the most amazing ways and has challenged me to grow in new and different ways, it's Bethany. For all of life's important moments as well as the daily grind, Bethany has been present. She is my sister from another mother, who is 22 years and counting of deep sista girl friendship. And, she is both figuratively and literally family—I introduced her to my cousin, who she married!

My friendship with Ayanna blossomed when I moved to Chicago in 2008 to attend business school. However, in my second year of business school, I broke up with the boyfriend that I had thought I was going to marry. One of the main reasons I went to business school in Chicago was to be with him, so you can imagine how devastating it was for me when we broke up.

Suddenly I found myself in a very lonely place. I eventually decided I'd had enough of loneliness, and I wanted some strong girl power in my life, someone who actually lived in the same city as me. I began praying for a good girlfriend. One day I was literally walking down the block back home from school and ran into Ayanna, who had been a classmate of mine at Yale. Until this time, we had been acquaintances, but we weren't close friends. I knew her on the surface, but I didn't really *know* her.

We talked a while and then said what people tend to say in such situations, "Hey, good to see you again. Let's catch up soon!" We parted, and I didn't think much about it until the next day we ended up connecting on Facebook. I was just in that spirit of having told the universe, "Man, I wish I had some good girlfriends." So when I saw her friend request, I decided, "Well, why don't I actually take her up on the offer to connect, and actually try and develop a relationship?"

We did that, and it turned out that Ayanna was also looking to develop some deeper relationships in her life because some of her really close friends were starting to have kids at the time, and if you are a parent like me, you know all about how kids can take time away from friendships. For the next five years, we were pretty inseparable. From dating our future husbands at the same time and enjoying so many outings, to going to the same church, and finding fun in Paris, we did life together in the most authentic of ways.

I also introduced Ayanna to her now-husband. Are you seeing a theme?

I've learned from my own experience: a critical factor in getting to know someone is no deeper than the fact that the timing is right. Both people have to be in a place where they have room for that kind of relationship, and it turned out that we did.

After establishing your initial foundations in friendship, you should have a strong base to work from. In my own case, Michelle, Bethany, and Ayanna were all in my wedding, not simply as bridesmaids, but properly titled "Sisters of the Spirit," along with three others: Phoebe, Jeanette, and Benasha. All of these beautiful women have a unique role in my life, and two of them are my cousins so I keep it in the family. There are too many stories and memories to share in this book about these women, as I'm sure you have with your friends.

But I share these stories with you to point out that once you put a desire to make new friends into your consciousness, then once you take action, you'll know early on whether or not this person has room for you and if you have room for them. You must then build mutual respect for one another. In our current society, there is more of a focus on making connections rather than friendships. I want you to have strong friendships.

When you're thinking about being a Wealthy Girl, you should explore creating friendships regularly. As I shared from the beginning of this book, attaining a wealth status includes building strong support networks of friends and family in your life—people who care about you personally, professionally, and spiritually. They should want the best for you and you should want the best for them. This holistic approach to wealth will create a solid foundation for you and your network will begin to flow naturally.

In the words of Olympic medalist skater Michelle Kwan, "If you have nothing in life but a good friend, you're rich." I definitely believe that, but I'd change the rich to wealthy. And Kwan is a great example of a Wealthy Girl in all areas of her life. It's critical to reach the understanding that life is all about people first and foremost, and it's also the quality of the people in your life that makes a difference.

Go find, and hold onto those—especially your female friends, family, and colleagues in your life with whom you can increase your respective and collective wealth. Start today to gain more for your tomorrows.

Chapter Takeaways

Building a wealthy environment takes an admission that you *need* a wealthy environment. Trust me, you should want one and you should have one. You deserve the benefits that come with that wealthy environment. Figure out who is going to build you up in love, help you practice ambition, and sit on the other side of a long-lasting female bond.

Because our brains are made up of neural networks, I have often found that by asking the following question, it helps me to focus and accelerate my wealthy potential:

Who's one person in your life
that you truly admire?

Do you admire them because of their ambition? What can you learn from their approach to life? Is this someone you think would have time to start a friendship where you could support one another in all the ways of Wealthy Girls—in prosperity, peace, and personal power? Tell that person how you feel and I think you'll be surprised by the power of your honesty. And make sure you're honest with yourself as to whether you are able to make the time to invest in this relationship. Like anything, strong friendships take effort.

When you ask this question from a point of being still, whether just before or after prayer or meditation, you typically will receive an answer that contains a really good choice for that potential new friend. Your "neural network sorting net" really goes to work for you and brings back a quality response. Then it's up to you to take action on it. From that point on, you can continue to nurture your friendship circle, focusing on quality rather than quantity.

You got this!

Step 1: Build an Environment for Wealth Creation (Part B)

I<small>N</small> C<small>HAPTER</small> 3, <small>WE</small> talked about how important it is to build a network of supportive people, whether family members or friends. Creating a wealthy environment, however, also entails expanding your circle of support beyond your immediate family and friend circle. The following is what my journey looked like.

When I reached my junior year in high school, I began seriously evaluating a variety of colleges. As I mentioned in Chapter 1, my Grandma Shine valued education and wanted her children to attend college because she was stripped of the opportunity to attend. Grandma passed on the value of education to my mother as one of the best intangible wealth assets you can have. Both parents instilled in me the desire to go to college. And since my brother had gone to college at SUNY Albany three years prior to me, I had good examples to follow. Surprisingly though, my school choice was influenced by someone other than a family member. I wound up going to Yale, as I mentioned briefly in Chapter 2, but that certainly was very, very far from where I originally thought I would attend.

I remember getting ready for the PSATs and the college application process. My guidance counselor had me make a list of all the schools to which I wanted to apply. My list included schools like Fordham University, NYU, and of course, SUNY Albany, where my brother attended. I added some historically Black colleges and universities to the list because my older cousins went there. When I finished I felt I had a well-rounded list of good schools, but I mulled over the list, again and again, for more than a month before I presented it to my guidance counselor.

My guidance counselor's immediate response was, "This is a good list." But about a week later, Mr. Kight, my basketball coach, who also happened to be an assistant principal, called me aside to touch base with me on my college plans. He was not only the coach to the girls on the basketball floor, but also vested in the success of all his players off the court.

When he got hold of my list, his feedback was, "These schools are okay. I mean, they're good. but they're not great. Charisse, your GPA is actually among the highest in your class. I'm just curious, why aren't there any Ivy League schools on this list?" Funny enough, Mr. Kight's prediction for my high school ranking was correct. To my surprise and great honor and appreciation, I eventually graduated as class salutatorian.

However, to his comment on pursuing an Ivy League school, I replied, "Well, those are for snobs and rich people. I don't fit there. Those schools have students who aren't down to earth." He gave me a serious look as he calmly stated, "With your grades, you will graduate valedictorian or salutatorian. You will graduate with that ranking because of your hard work. You're involved in so many things: sports, service, bands, tutoring. That caliber of school needs you, and you absolutely deserve to be there."

He went on to ask me, "Have you visited any of them?" to which I answered, "No." He insisted that I add a few Ivies to my list, so it expanded to include Columbia, Yale, Harvard, and the "Ivies of the South": the University of Virginia, Georgetown, and Duke.

I wound up applying to all of the schools on my revised list, and I got into every single one, with the exception of Harvard. The initial rejection hurt, even though my mother reminds me that I submitted a half-hearted application. In my heart, I was actually glad I didn't get in there because after I visited the campus, I realized it wasn't the right fit for me. However, I learned an important lesson in getting rejected from Harvard: when one door closes for me, it makes attractive the doors that are open. All I have to do is believe in the legitimacy of the open door, and that I am uniquely qualified to accept what's on the other side.

Interestingly enough, I applied to Yale prior to being able to visit the campus with my parents. When I first set foot onto that campus, it opened up for me an aha moment of, "Wow! What an experience." After that visit I found myself hoping and praying to get admitted there. Walking through the campus I was in awe. I met students who were just like me—smart, down to earth, and looked like me—people who genuinely cared about the world around them. I realized that this environment was perfect for me and that I did belong at Yale.

Thankfully, I got my acceptance letter a few months later.

The joy of getting in was ephemeral. I wasn't awarded any financial aid because my family was stuck in the middle of the qualification range, nor did I get an athletic scholarship. This meant that my parents would have to pay out of pocket. I was both devastated and frustrated at the stark reality that many middle-class families find themselves in. I carried the weight of our situation in my heart for many, many years as it left a profound impact on how I viewed access and opportunity.

Gratefully, my parents removed the large financial burden of college by making it theirs to carry. They said to me simply, "I guess we're all going to Yale. We'll make the investment. This kind of opportunity does not come along often for our family." They ended up getting a second mortgage on their home to finance my college education, and both of my parents picked up second jobs. In turn,

I made the commitment to work each of my four years throughout the school year and each summer in between in order to contribute what I could to finance books, a portion of my tuition, and other expenses.

My parents believed in me and my right to go to Yale. So it was with a deep, collective commitment that we joined forces as a unit, pooling our resources and leveraging access to their home equity in order to make my dreams come true.

I will always be grateful to my parents for the sacrifices they made on my behalf, and I'll always be thankful that Mr. Kight made it his personal business to make me think differently and strive for the stars. You should know that Mr. Kight is Black, and this mattered in my journey. I needed someone who looked like me *and* had a position of authority in my high school to make me believe that I would fit at Yale. In doing so, he helped change the trajectory of my life, not just in getting a great education from Yale, but also establishing beautiful relationships that emanated from that experience and shaping my first notions on wealth. I am still in touch with Mr. Kight to this day. He showed up at my baby shower in 2019, beaming with the same pride at the birth of my first child as he did when he attended my graduation from Yale in 2002.

Your A-Team

As you think about your own journey, start by looking at the people you have around you daily, weekly, or monthly, beyond your family and friends. I call this expanded circle your A-Team. As a young adult, Mr. Kight was part of my A-Team. This is a compilation of people who are vested in your success and can change the trajectory of your life. These people can include informal peer groups, mentors, sponsors, coaches, financial advisors, and even therapists. You may not have all of these A-Team members at the same time, but they can be extremely important in different seasons in your life. Your A-Team can catapult you on a path to become a Wealthy Girl.

Your A-Team is there to assist you in being your best self, which is when you are able to pursue wealth in its fullest form.

I want to put a frame around this by asking, "What's wrong with an assist?" The answer is—nothing. As I mentioned before, I played basketball through high school. There I learned early that to give yourself a shot at winning the game you must put the ball in the basket. Everyone loves the players who can shoot the ball well. But there's also the teammate who passes the ball that allows the shooter to send it into the hoop. That kind of teamwork creates an assist for the player who passed the ball to the person who makes the basket. Michael Jordan, one of the greatest basketball players of all time, in the 2020 documentary *The Last Dance,* talked expressively about how he could only shine the way he did because he was assisted by his teammates.

Your A-Team offers you the assistance to shine in your life. No one gets great by themselves. By fostering an A-team around you, you have others committed to your success. The concept of assistance from an A-Team might feel countercultural. In American culture and other Western cultures around the world, we pride ourselves on individualized achievement, which can make one feel that assists are bad. But when I look at people I admire who have achieved success on their own terms, every one of them benefited from the different types of A-Team members that I have shared with you. Sometimes it's not until you talk with people who have used professional advisors and find out, "Oh, wow! This person had all this help!" that you begin to uncover the secret of their success is the result of a professional's help.

Remember Myth 8 from Chapter 2: wealth is a result of one's individual achievements? Well, your A-Team defies that myth in its fullest form. This is because it represents one of the secrets of the wealthy:

Wealthy people do not get wealthy solely because of their individual efforts.

They hire or build friendships with a team of experts, confidants, and champions who have made it their business to make these people wealthy. So how can you accomplish something similar?

Well, I will show you. I now want to share a breakdown of each of the different types of supporters and the value that each can bring to help you achieve your wealth goals.

Form Informal Peer Groups

The best peer groups I have discovered and become a part of have emerged outside of traditional structures. In other words, they haven't been confined to preexisting structures or require that you formally apply in order to gain access to them. Note, however, that informal does not mean unstructured; informal means they have a more relaxed environment than some of the formal peer groups. Nonetheless, informal peer groups can become an important part of your A-team.

Then there are formal peer groups. I've had the good fortune of applying to, and getting accepted into, formal peer groups and networks such as INROADs, Management Leadership for Tomorrow, and Toigo. All of these groups were founded for the benefit of people of color, given the systemic ways white dominant culture often makes it difficult for us to access internships and full-time job opportunities in corporate America. These programs provided extensive training, comprehensive programming, formal mentorship, and peer networks to help me develop into a future leader in the world.

These more traditional structures choose the peers in your network for you, in hopes of creating cohorts of like-minded individuals marching toward a broad goal, such as getting a collegiate business internship as in INROADs, pursuing a master's in business administration, as in Management Leadership for Tomorrow, or excelling as a leader in your career, as in Toigo. These formal peer networks have been instrumental and valuable in their own right, and you should surely aspire to be part of networks like these to achieve your objectives. Given their selective and often prescriptive nature, however, informal peers groups can be a nice complement or alternative.

For the purpose of informal peer groups, I define peers as people who have similar aspirations to yours around the same time. Peers don't have to be in the same age range, but rather in the same life or career stage, wherein they are trying to accomplish a similar goal at around the same time as you are. Some of your peers might be a little more ahead, maybe like six months, or a little behind where you might be in your journey. The key here is that you're basically in the same stage so that there's mutual benefit. This way, every person will feel that they are going to get something out of being in an intentional relationship with their peers—the essence of a true peer group.

In my own experience, these informal peer groups are formed out of necessity and creativity to meet your specific needs where traditional or structured peer groups may fall short. Involvement in these informal peer groups has led me to some of my most meaningful relationships, in part because we co-crafted, co-inspired, and held each other accountable to a shared vision that *we* created.

Peer groups by nature tend to foster a system of mutual support, so that everyone does have a vested interest in the success of the others in the group. If you are interested in this type of group, you can join an existing group or start your own if none exists to meet your needs. If you are joining an existing group, you may find out about them online, in a church setting, or by asking your friends or colleagues if they are aware of any groups that meet your needs.

If you are starting your own group, begin by compiling a list of four to five potential people to join you. Once you compile the list, share your idea with one of the people on the list to get some quick feedback and see whether the idea for the peer group resonates with them. Move down the list and when you have two people ready to go, you're ready to start your peer group. If you are invited to join a peer group, evaluate whether the group meets your needs. If you discover that there isn't one that meets your schedule or specific purpose, create one that works for you. It only takes two people to start a group. Peer groups should only require time, and not any monetary investment or commitment on your part.

I'll share two examples of informal peer groups that I've participated in, how they got started, and the value in each type. Informal peer groups often do not last forever, but rather for life seasons. I believe that naming groups is extremely important, as the name conveys and carries the energy of the group for that moment in time. These two examples have enriched my life in multiple ways, and I share them with you to give you an idea of how peer groups can enrich your life too because of the wealth effect—both intangible and tangible—that they create.

SIM (Smaller in Manhattan, 2004–10)

My faith has always been extremely important to me. When I lived in Brooklyn after college, I found a home church called Emmanuel Baptist Church in Fort Greene, about a twenty-five minute walk from my apartment in Park Slope on Sundays. My church, however, was about a forty-five minute to an hour train ride from where I worked in Manhattan. I wanted to be part of a "small group," the name given to groups where people gather to study the Bible together and share about their lives in a more intimate environment. These small groups are in essence peer groups, as I defined earlier. But attending one of the church's established weeknight small groups proved to be tough, given that they all started at six p.m. and I normally worked until that time. So these groups were a nonstarter for me because by the time I'd arrive, it would be over.

But I still wanted to be part of that kind of community of faith in a small group. Bethany, my sister from another mother who I talked about in Chapter 3, also lived with me in Brooklyn, wanted the same thing. We attended the same church, and she also worked in Manhattan. So there were commonalities to our schedule and a few of the things that we wanted. I also had started a book club with Bethany right after college, so we had the experience of starting something fun together.

That's why when I said to myself, "Hey, I want to do something that's different outside of church that's still connected to the church," who did I look to? I looked to the same person that I started a really fun book club with, and who also cares deeply about her faith. We approached the church and said, "Hey, we want to start this new group," and after some initial resistance, they said, "Okay! We'll also assign you a deacon." Deacon Sheryl only attended meetings upon our invitation. We called on her like a lifeline when we wanted some spiritual guidance or help in facilitating difficult conversations. As you think about your peer group, evaluate whether you need an expert or guest who can add value to your peer group at specific moments in time.

We eventually called ourselves SIM, which stands for Smaller in Manhattan. We started this group in 2004, and met weekly until 2010. The group normally stayed anywhere between eight and ten people so it was small in nature. I know that there are some really big peer groups in a variety of areas, but personally I have found the most profound ones to be around eight to ten people in any given meeting. Sometimes my SIM group was only four people, so they can get smaller, too.

We started with people from the same church who also worked in Manhattan or lived far from the church.

Outside of my friend Bethany, I did not know anyone else on a deep level at the outset. But we all mostly had corporate jobs, so again there was that similarity in what we were going through in our day-to-day lives. Eventually, though, the group expanded to include people who didn't go to our church, because those who did would often invite other people who they thought would benefit.

We studied the Bible together, shared life experiences, and eventually celebrated life milestones together. One of the books that we read together is *Spiritual Disciplines for Christian Living*, which I still reference today. The book has been transformative to fostering several disciplines, including journaling, tithing, praying, and fasting. Because I read the book within my SIM group, we were able to hold each other accountable. I would not have been as diligent or been able to stick to some of the disciplines had we not been doing it together. That is the power of the peer group. I believe that you have a higher level of accountability because you do not want to disappoint your peers.

When I left New York City in 2008 to go to business school, another SIM member took over running the group. I knew that she could take over running the group and make sure people stayed accountable to each other. She continued to lead the group for two more years, which is important because here's something that's unique about peer groups: they need a leader and organizer to make sure that the members and the structure stay together.

Sometimes in peer groups, you can take turns being the leader. You can designate someone to coordinate and appropriately structure the group to ensure that the peer group stays in the communication loop and that the goals of the group are met.

SIM was incredibly instrumental in elevating my understanding of the value of informal peer groups for personal growth. Peer support is a wonderful way to join with like-minded people as you all work on your individual passions. Having others to bounce ideas off of and brainstorm with can motivate you in a different and more accountable manner.

Black Power, Entrepreneurs Circle (2010–15)

The second informal peer group that I became involved in served a more professional purpose. We eventually assumed the name Black Power, Entrepreneurs Circle (BPEC). In 2010, I officially launched Smarteys, my financial technology company, which you will hear more about in Chapter 8. The idea for a new peer group hit me when I realized, "Hey! I need some fellow entrepreneurs who actually look like me and have similar experiences and challenges that we can discuss openly." Prior to forming BPEC, the predominantly white entrepreneurial circles that I had been frequenting always left me yearning for more, especially since I did not feel that I could fully be myself as a Black entrepreneur.

So I reached out to my friend and fellow Chicago Booth recent graduate Seyi Fabode, who was starting his own utility business, Power2Switch (later purchased by Choose Energy), to see if he wanted to be part of an informal entrepreneur group together. When we talked, he had already been working on Power2Switch for some time, and his start-up pursuit was about six months ahead of mine. The fact that he was also a person of color mattered. While his experience growing up in Nigeria differed from my upbringing in the United States, we both felt the systemic effects of being Black in America: lack of access to venture capital funding for our technology companies, being shut out from white-dominated entrepreneurial networks and circles that would have helped us make seismic traction in our businesses, and a feeling that we faced higher standards than our white counterparts. For the very first time, Seyi had discovered that he was not getting the traction that he wanted in his business, in part, because of the color of his skin. As such, Seyi also felt the need to be in a group where he could learn from others, share resources, and be comfortable. Seyi said "yes" to the group. We invited our respective Black co-founders and several other Black entrepreneurs to join us.

We launched the group because we felt locked out of certain existing circles, yet our group became *the circle* that we aspired to be a part of relative to the others. Our informal peer group met on a weekly basis, and later on a monthly basis, to hold each other accountable and push each other toward very specific milestones and deliverables. That's why the naming of the group was so important for us; we named ourselves Black Power, Entrepreneurs Circle because in the circle, we could not be removed from each other. We were all Black entrepreneurs who created space for ourselves to connect and grow. In doing so, we gave ourselves the power and authority to do what we needed to do to be successful, defined on our own terms.

We shared resources—lawyers, potential funders, marketing strategies and firms, office space—to grow our respective businesses and bring others along with us. In its original rendition, BPEC lasted from 2010 to 2015. We saw anywhere from ten to fifteen people in a given month during our most active years. As our numbers grew, it was a clear indication to other Black entrepreneurs that they could join us and meet in a space where they could also be vulnerable. We made a commitment to not only helping each other excel, but also sowing the seeds for our members to serve as volunteers and instructors in other entrepreneurial settings.

BPEC is also a prime example of an informal peer group that resurfaced years later in a new construct. As I wrote this book in 2020, a former BPEC member decided to relaunch the group. After some initial hesitancy given the different demands on my time, including motherhood, I eventually agreed to be part of the journey. Since many of us have gotten married, now have children, and live in different locations than we did then, we have found a way to adjust our formation to meet our new realities.

Today, we meet virtually every other month to push forward our respective entrepreneurial endeavors, and we have taken an even more acute focus on helping other Black entrepreneurs be successful. While we are bound by the original BPEC purpose, we certainly have brought new learnings, new challenges, and new opportunities.

An informal peer group like BPEC may serve a similar purpose in your professional journey, especially if you have subscribed to the myth that "There is only a select group of wealthy, white people" that I discussed in Chapter 2. Forming an informal peer group that circumvents traditional access points is a tried-and-tested strategy to build acceptance and wealth among like-minded individuals as well as those who may look like you.

Are you feeling the desire to join with other peers toward a common goal? If you already have an informal peer group, your group may need to morph in order to meet the needs of your peers. From my own experience, a new formation can be a welcome change.

Regardless of what type of informal peer group you consider for yourself, the most important aspect is to allow it to create wealth for your life.

Secure Mentors and Sponsors, and Know the Difference

Informal peer groups play their own role in your profes-sional and personal development, but mentors and sponsors play another important, yet individualized role. At some point, everyone needs a *great* mentor, and should experience the power of an effective sponsor. I have been the beneficiary of both, and they are irreplaceable. Furthermore, if you have the capacity and desire, you should consider being a mentor and sponsor to others so you can pass the wealth forward.

Let me first define a mentor in my own terms, and then share what makes a great one. Mentors are individuals who provide advice and guidance in your life, potentially on the job. Mentors can be the same age as you, or younger or older, but they have one thing in common regardless of age: some type of experience, success, or skill set that you desire to possess or learn. You tend to go to a mentor when you have a specific challenge or opportunity and you seek their counsel.

My great mentors have emerged organically, starting with me reaching out to get to know someone better, and then the relationship evolving over time into a beautiful mentor-mentee relationship. I have found these mentors in a variety of places, including on the job, at conferences, or through a connection from a mutual connection. After my initial reach out, I gained a better understanding of who they are as people and what I could potentially learn from them as well as offer them.

Eventually, this person got to know me too, and he or she developed an interest in helping me achieve a particular goal or help me develop as a person. At some point in our conversations, I made a specific ask of that person to mentor me. I simply said, "I know you've been mentoring me informally for these several months, and I want to ask if you would consider being my official mentor?" With my great mentor relationships, we have been very transparent and intentional about the nature of our relationship.

We have agreed to a specific cadence to meet, and then I was responsible for setting up those times. I have found that forming relationships in this manner, rather than being preassigned to a mentor through a program or on the job, has resulted in much stronger and longer-lasting bonds.

My best mentors have also played that particular role for a specific period of time, and yours might also serve in a mentorship capacity only for a season. During these periods, my best mentors have challenged my thinking, provided me with alternative perspectives, opened their networks, and shared relevant lessons that they have drawn from their own or others' experiences.

Great mentors usually know they have a lot to offer, and thus everyone wants to be their mentee and they are super busy. Find a way to make your relationship special, and ask how you can structure the relationship so that it fits in their schedule. One effective strategy I have used to make our relationship mutually fruitful with great mentors who are busy is to send periodic updates between our in-person or telephone meetings. Over time, mentors know your dreams and goals and become vested in your success.

One of the keys to a great mentor-mentee relationship is that it's reciprocal, and thus you should not underestimate what you have to offer your mentor, be it a renewed spirit, personal satisfaction in helping you, or something very tangible that you can help them accomplish. If you do not have any ideas on what your reciprocity can look like, you can take this approach: "I'm so grateful to you for helping me. Is there anything I can offer you in return? If nothing comes to mind now, please think about it." You are on your way toward a strong mentor-mentee relationship that has the potential to create a magnitude of wealth in your life. One final word of caution: if you are not inspired by your mentor or don't feel there is mutual respect, then get a new one. I say this because there must be something about him or her that keeps you coming back to be in their presence, and him or her wanting to come back in yours. If not, your relationship may fizzle out or you may not be as fulfilled in your relationship as you originally intended.

In addition to mentors, I recommend that you find an effective *sponsor* at your job. A sponsor is someone who will use their platform, position, or power to advance your goals and ambitions. A sponsor puts their personal reputation on the line for your advancement, which can come in the form of a promotion, a coveted project opportunity, or a leadership position. A sponsor is also comfortable with the potential risk that you might fail en route to your advancement. In essence, you are given the freedom to fail and experiment due to their sponsorship and ultimately their reputation.

Effective sponsors tend to find mutual benefit in their relationship with you. For example, a sponsor might put your name in the hat for a promotion, and if you get the promotion, the sponsor might directly benefit from you sitting in a higher-level position. Effective sponsorship typically comes with plenty of resources, both financial and nonfinancial (e.g., social capital, extensive time, and access to their networks) to ensure that your goals are met. Sponsorship is different from mentorship because sponsorship has a more direct impact on your career path. Sponsors make a commitment to fundamentally change the trajectory of your career or life. I think effective sponsors treat you similarly to how they would like someone to treat their own child; sponsors put the time and brand equity into ensuring your success by taking you under their wing.

Unlike mentors who you choose, sponsors usually must choose you. A sponsor must choose to elevate their role in your career. That said, you can also ask someone directly at certain points to sponsor a circumstance or situation, and that may lead to a longer-term sponsorship relationship. I'm not going to lie—securing an effective sponsor is difficult because the sponsor must find you. If your mentor sits in a position of authority at your job, he or she could become a good candidate for your sponsor down the line. In Chapter 5 I will share the impactful story of how one of my mentors turned into a sponsor who influenced me to get the credentials necessary to become a respected investor.

Overall, I have benefited from both mentors and sponsors, and these relationships have enriched my life. I want the same for you.

Invest in a Coach

While informal peer groups, mentors, and sponsors provide excellent opportunities to expand your circle of support, these relationships typically come with no financial cost to you. Your professional and personal progress can be heightened even further with a formal coach who you pay for their individualized support of you. Coaches can play such an integral role on your A-Team. I wish someone would have told me about the power of coaches when I was in my twenties. I feel that coaches are the best-kept secret for those who aspire toward greatness. As I have spent time with more and more wealthy individuals, I have learned that many of them have benefited from a professional coach, whether a career, executive, or life coach.

Behind every great athlete is a superb coach, and you can draw that same parallel to your own journey. Interestingly enough, when I first started hearing people talk about coaches, at first my question was, "Why do I need a coach?" Then as I learned more, the question morphed into, "Who's your coach, and what type do you have?" I got a career coach at the end of 2013, and it has been one of the best investments I've ever made in my career. Honestly, no one in my professional circle had a career coach, or they kept it a secret if they did have one. The first time I heard one of my friends talk about a career coach was when I began contemplating shutting down my company, Smarteys, in early 2013.

This friend had used a career coach after selling her business. She wanted to create a new role for herself that would allow her to spend time with her young kids and yet satisfy her desire to have a fruitful career. My eyes lit up when I heard about her coach because I needed someone to help me get clarity on a potential next move and navigate a transition. I was shutting down my business and trying to get out of a state of depression at the same time. My goals included building myself back up professionally and I wanted some guidance and coaching around that.

So I had several questions:

- What would I do if I wasn't running a start-up, and will my skills translate?
- Would I find as much joy in this next phase of my professional life?
- How much money did I want to support my lifestyle?

And, I still wanted to dream big!

My friend told me to give her a call for an initial and free consultation, and so I did. When the coach told me that she never met with her clients in person but rather over the phone, I thought we would never work together because I always envisioned meeting someone face-toface. Boy, was I wrong.

You may not click with the first career coach you meet, but if you do, go with it. After working with my coach for over a year and a half, I've discovered these facts to be true for me. Perhaps they will hold true for you too. A career coach will help you grow. A career coach is part coach, part counselor or therapist, and part mentor for your professional well-being. It all depends on their background. For example, they may specialize in a specific industry, while others specialize in helping their clients work through transitions or handle difficult situations. If you are at an executive level (based on your title at work) some career coaches specialize strictly in executive coaching.

But I have also found value in using a career coach in a post-transition phase, too. Your career coach is someone who is vested in your professional success, understands your values, and sees that you are not just your career, but that you are a whole person with life goals. Yes!

A career coach can provide objective advice and tactics and strategies (e.g., email reviews, negotiating salary, perks, reviews of your resume, etc.) to take you to the next level in your career. Over time, she or he will know your story, but will not be emotionally tied to you like your spouse or a close friend. Your close circle of family and friends are great resources, but they know you personally and so they are biased and may want to give you advice that might or might not be right for you.

Ask any potential career coach why she or he is doing their job. Their answers will provide insight into what motivates them. Your goal is to find someone passionate about helping others realize their biggest career goals.

The financial investment is real. Career coaches are not cheap and can cost anywhere from $100 to $200 and even up to $500 per hour. Many coaches need at least three one-hour sessions to find out about you and go through exercises and assessments with you, so plan accordingly. (With many online platforms today such as CoachHub.com[16] and Careerwave.me[17] the price of coaching has dropped dramatically.) Or your employer might offer coaching services as a perk.

I personally have used coaching from Valorperform. com, a hybrid platform that provides one-on-one leadership coaching plus self-directed digital learning that my employer paid for me to use. If your employer does not offer this perk, you can encourage your employer to offer it in the future. Never underestimate the power of your voice in asking for what you want.

Remember, however, to be clear with yourself about what you are expecting in return for their services: a higher-paying job or more income at your current job, peace of mind at work, support to finally go after your dreams, next-level professional development. Framed this way, paying now for a career coach should reap long-term returns for your career. I am a big proponent in paying for quality and getting a return on my investment. You get what you put in, so if you are not ready to take advantage of what career coaches can offer, then you will not reap a big return on your investment.

Ask the career coach to explain their approach to your situation and describe some tangible takeaways that you will receive from working with her or him. For example, my coach asked me to list every job, paid and unpaid, that I have worked. She then asked me to write down what I liked and did not like about each of these jobs. I discovered that I love using my creativity to execute on ideas but hate the redundancy and administration of routine tasks. Through this exercise my coach helped me discover my values and the type of work that aligns well with them.

By working with a coach your inner confidence will jump to a new level. I'm sure you are a confident person if you're reading about how to get to the next level in your career. Working with a career coach, however, can give you a deeper connection to yourself and eventually make you more confident in your skills and your value to the world. Unexpected work difficulties or past work failures can break the spirit of even the most confident people you know. Alternatively, work successes and achievements can cause a level of contentment for overachievers. Regardless of the end of the spectrum you fall in, a good career coach will force you to evaluate *why* you make (or refrain from) certain work decisions. You will be in tune with your own inner compass.

A great career coach will also remind you that work is what you do, not who you *are*. She will push you to be your best whole self, recognizing that if you have other emotional or physical stuff that you need to work out, it will be hard to advance in your career. If you are not doing a lot of self-introspection with your coach, then alarm bells should be going off in your head. Run quickly and find someone else who pushes you to this level.

Your career coach will hold you accountable to hitting milestones, just like a physical trainer. And in the process, you will sharpen your intuition and handle difficult situations much more effectively. Alternatively, if you're successful in what you do already but are not hitting your desired level of achievement, a good career coach can help steer you in the way that you should be growing.

Regardless of where you fall on that spectrum, career coaches will force you to evaluate why you made certain decisions in your career. Ultimately, this will enable you to be in tune with your inner conflict and really understand how to resolve it and emerge with a higher level of self-respect.

My advice is, whether you're stuck in your current career or want to take it to the next level, definitely consider investing in a career coach. If you are financially constrained, don't be shy about asking your potential career coach if he or she has any special packages or arrangements to meet you where you are financially.

Be patient and recognize that it may take six months to a year to see tangible results. I'm here to assure you though that after that amount of time, you will look back and have your own breakthrough story to tell.

Invest in a Therapist as You Need

Say this word out loud: *therapist.* Yes. And say it again with me: *therapist.* You may be wondering why therapists are finding their way into this wealth book. I'll quickly break it down for you. When I say therapist, I mean someone who is professionally trained to help you deal with your stuff. Everyone has stuff they are dealing with. Do not let the outward smiles fool you; inwardly, most people are dealing with something in one form or another.

I'm not talking about the therapy you will undoubtedly get from your family and friends, which is biased in your direction. With a professional therapist, you have an objective space to deal with blockages, life transitions (e.g., marriage, parenting, career move, etc.) or challenges, and more importantly, prepare you for future opportunity.

Working with therapists potentially provides an envi-ronment for you to grow personally. The thing that many people underestimate is how much your issues can weigh you down in your pursuit of wealth. If you haven't dealt with issues that might be lurking underneath the surface, then it is incredibly difficult to spend the time or energy on wealth-building activities. Think of a therapist, then, as part of your A-Team to create an environment that fosters wealth-creation. Good therapists specialize in helping you remove the things blocking you from moving forward in life.

Ask yourself this simple question: Do I have something going on in my life that prevents me from being my best self or fulfilling my purpose?

If the answer is "yes," then you should consider finding a therapist to help you be your best self.

A therapists' professional background matters. As you evaluate whether a therapist works for you, find out whether the therapist is a licensed counselor, licensed social worker, psychiatrist, or psychologist. You also must recognize the specific need that you have when you are seeking the right therapist. Some therapists specialize in particular clientele. For example, they may only work with women, or families, or couples.

I have worked with a therapist for the past five years, and it's proven to be incredibly impactful given the many challenges and transitions I've experienced over the years. Therapy is an outlet for my inner self, and I think as a woman (and definitely as a woman of color), we are socialized to take on that burden of shouldering so much for our families and our communities. Trust me, it's tiring.

One of my clients sent me a message that I now keep to remind me of the burden that I often carry. It reads: "She is strong, but she is exhausted." As such, a therapist can definitely help to lighten the exhaustion. My therapist has really helped to hold my issues with me, and work with me to develop strategies to handle my stuff. Therapy does take effort, which can lead to self-discovery, which can range from liberating, surprising, confusing, and painful, to everything in between.

Over time, therapy can become a great form of selfcare, including emotional and mental health—a huge intangible asset. Just like you go to the doctor's office or gym to preserve your physical health, you can go to a therapist for mental and emotion restoration.

Therapy can provide a constant outlet to help you process what's going on in your life. And if you're like me and have a lot going on, soak up the opportunity to have someone assist you in sorting through it all. I've discovered that therapy also helps remove the emotional burden I place on friends or family, which then gives us the room to focus on other things like having fun. Going to therapy is preventative health. If you give it time and focus, it becomes routine and part of your journey. In my life, I have found therapy to be that mental and emotional wellness check-in that creates a healthy, wealth-giving mindset thanks to inner reflection.

I've come to believe that the best time to seek out a great therapist is not always when you're in crisis and need help. While it's true that a personal crisis might be the initial impetus to see a therapist, a crisis should not be the reason that you keep going.

The frequency of your visits can vary. Sometimes, it's helpful to meet once a week, and other times, meeting once a month or even once a quarter might suffice. Evaluate what level of frequency works for you based upon what's going on in your life, what other things you are managing in your life, how much you need that extra support, and how much it costs. Therapy usually comes with a financial cost, even if most of it is covered by your health insurance plan. Even then, you still might pay out-of-pocket first through your deductible or a co-pay.

Again, consider your therapist as one member of your A-Team who can hold you accountable to the way in which you want to show up in this world. A good therapist will give you homework or make you reflect on a challenging situation in a whole new light. In its purest form, therapy will help provide an environment for you to be completely vulnerable and not hold back. As Brené Brown, one of my favorite authors and psychologists, tells us in *Rising Strong: How the Ability to Reset Transforms the Way We Live, Love, Parent, and Lead:*[18]

> *Vulnerability is not winning or losing; it's having the courage to show up and be seen when we have no control over the outcome. Vulnerability is not weakness; it's our greatest measure of courage.*

Now, I must admit that finding a great therapist will probably take some time, and you might have to go through a few that don't fit in the process of getting to a great one. If you're like me, you might even be a little uncomfortable asking someone in your circle of friends or family about a referral for a therapist. It's not the question you blurt out at the Thanksgiving table or over brunch. But you might offer up this inquiry when you're talking with a trusted friend: "Hey girl, I'm looking for a good therapist. By any chance can you recommend someone?" Once I started telling a few friends that I was looking for a therapist, I received an outpouring of love, support, and referrals. I said to myself ,"What took me so long?"

Alternatively, there are many new online therapy platforms such as Talkspace, BetterHelp, or TeenCounseling that have made the process of finding and engaging with a therapist much more effective. In some cases, the fees for these online services are a lot lower than some of the more traditional therapy services.

There is no shame in therapy. Better yet, my hope is that therapy gives you the confidence to go forth boldly and eventually tell others about the positive benefits you received. In this way, we can collectively crush the stigma and pass the wealth forward. Everybody deserves to find the best ways possible to show up in the world and fulfill their purpose. If a therapist helps you get there, why not try it out for yourself?

Invest in a Financial Advisor

You are almost done rounding out some key members of your A-Team. Now let's talk about financial advisors, because these are the individuals who will assist you the most in building tangible wealth. I think all of us eventually ask ourselves the question, "How do I get to the next level when it comes to managing my money and building tangible wealth?" Here's what I recommend: The first step is assuming a position of power over your wealth. I suggest that you begin by thinking of yourself as the CEO of your wealth. I will talk more about this mindset in Chapter 6. This is about treating your wealth like a business. If you've never been the CEO of a business, then this is your shot because it's the highest level of executive power. You are in charge of setting the vision of your wealth and your vision is all of the dreams and aspirations of the life that you want to have.

One thing that I have respected most about the great CEOs that I've worked closest with in my professional career is that they have intelligent and committed people on their management teams to assist them in making the company, and themselves, great. One critical management team role is a chief operating officer (COO). If you look at yourself as the CEO of your wealth, then consider your financial advisor as the COO of your wealth.

Your financial advisor, or COO of your wealth, has the professional experience to execute on your wealth strategy. They can act as a gatekeeper for you with regard to your wealth. Nothing reaches you unless it's vetted by your advisor. He or she acts as your wingwoman or wingman when it comes to helping you invest.

When you have a financial advisor who acts as the COO of your wealth, it causes you to recognize the benefits of pursuing wealth with a wealth expert at your side. Having an advisor who can help manage your wealth *on your behalf* is really important, especially when things go bad. And there will be times when your investments go south, or there is a dramatic shift in your life, like a divorce or job loss or unexpected medical expenses, for example. Financial advisors provide you with a check-in regarding your own vision for your wealth and money. So when times get tough or you get emotional about your wealth and your money, your financial advisor should be that even-keeled support partner who helps bolster you. They're the professional who will help keep you moving forward toward your goals.

A good financial advisor will also give you insights and access to good investment products and services, and that access is crucial. Here, they focus on buying stocks and mutual funds, or having a brokerage account or a good 401k retirement plan. But the cold hard truth is that you can't always get access to solid information or advice about mutual funds or investment products from brokerage firms on your own. In order to gain that access you actually have to have a lot of money, or you need a connection. If you hire a financial advisor who has an excellent track record in that arena, then there you go—they provide you with that hookup.

The major value proposition for securing a financial advisor is the organization and acceleration of your wealth pursuits. When you find the right financial advisor and commit to work with her or him, you are effectively stepping up your game and playing in an environment that will help you move farther, faster.

Professional financial advisors are charged with what is called a fiduciary responsibility to protect your money and make you more of it. The best ones usually have a series of letters indicating their credentials following their name. For instance, a CFP is a certified financial planner. A CFA is a chartered financial analyst, which I am; I will share more about my journey toward attaining that designation in Chapter 5.

You might be thinking, "Well, I already have a CPA, (certified public accountant) to do my taxes." But there are distinct differences between those designations. Unlike a CPA, a CFP or CFA has a fiduciary responsibility to ensure that you manage your money properly. So it's important that you look for those credentials. One of the best ways to find the right financial advisor or planner is to get referrals. Sound familiar to my advice earlier in the chapter? It is. Look around your circle of friends and colleagues. Ask them who they use and how that's been working out.

Lastly, it's important to have a clear understanding of exactly how much a financial advisor is going to cost you. You have to have the wherewithal to work with them. Some financial planners charge commissions, which is a fee you pay whenever investment products or financial instruments are bought or sold. Personally, I don't like commissions because they're expensive or give the planner incentive to sell them. Bottom line? The more commission-based products they sell you, the more money they get, and these products may not always be in your own best interest. In Chapter 6, I'll talk more about other types of financial advisors, such as robo-advisors that have attempted to reduce the cost of financial planning.

For now, consider a financial advisor as an important member of your A-Team. As the COO of your wealth, they have a vested interest in seeing your wealth grow.

Chapter Takeaways

Your A-Team can take on many forms, from informal peers in a group, to coaches, to mentors and sponsors, to therapists, to financial advisors. Depending on where you are in your own journey, you may want or need only one, or all of them. I want you to answer the following questions:

- *Who needs to be on your A-team at this moment in your life?*
- *Is there anyone who you have given A-team status who needs to be removed from this position of power?*

I believe that the journey matters even more than the destination. Being willing to expand your circle of support will help you grow as an individual. Because these people in your orbit will be able to bring some or all of your blind spots to light. Their doing so will motivate you to push not only toward your purpose and your goals, but also toward your well-being and personal power faster and in a deeper, richer way than you probably would have on your own.

I will end as I began, with the wisdom of my Grandma Shine, "Why go at it alone when you can bring someone else with you?" That's what you can achieve when you build your A-Team. Your ideal A-Team will be made up of people who will expand beyond your original notion of what it means to have others support you.

Go get your A-Team, and create your wealthy environment.

5

Step 2: Work Your Craft

IN STEP 1, I provided you with strategies to create an environment for wealth creation. Now, I want to share with you the powerful step of working your craft in order to help you build a prosperous life. Your craft is one of your most precious intangible assets—it is worth something of great value and contributes to your personal wealth.

I first worked on one of my crafts—my investing craft—after graduating from Yale, when I started my career at J. P. Morgan as a junior client portfolio specialist in 2002. In my job, I supported the senior client portfolio specialist team in managing client relationships with institutions whose money J. P. Morgan managed.

At the time, the J. P. Morgan investment team managed approximately $40 billion in U.S. equity assets, or investments in the U.S. stock market. For reference, other types of assets include investments such as bonds, real estate, venture capital, and private equity.) We played the role of the customer service reps in the asset management group, and thus institutional clients came to us to find answers to their questions, understand what's happening in the U.S. stock market overall, and get updates on their portfolio of investments. In simple terms, I was an account manager for institutions with millions of dollars held at our firm.

It took me about a year to understand that managing investments on behalf of clients took an entire team beyond the client portfolio specialists like me. The team included investors—the ones making the decisions on where to invest client money—and salespeople who are trying to sell new investment products to clients. These investors and salespeople augmented the role of client specialists like me so that the client had a full team of support.

Twelve months into working in my client specialist role, I knew that I eventually wanted to be in an investor role. I didn't want to stay in a client service role; I wanted to be *making* the decisions on where clients should invest their money, particularly in the U.S. stock market. During that same time, I received my first review.

At the time, we were reviewed on a scale of 1, 2, or 3:

- 1 is outstanding—your performance is above average among your peers.
- 2 is good—your performance is average among your peers.

- 3 is poor—your performance is below average among your peers.

At my very first review, my manager told me that I was ranked a 2. I was shocked! I'd never been an average performer. The alarming thing was that I thought that I was performing well above average. What this assessment taught me is that sometimes there is a disconnect between where you think you're performing and where you're actually performing. If you find yourself in this predicament, get clarity quickly.

At that very same time, I made it pretty clear to my manager that I no longer wanted to be on the client side of the house, but on the investment side. But the feedback I received then was, "Well, Charisse, if you're an average performer, then it might be very difficult for you to move over to another area. And note that there is a waiting list of people looking to join an investment team. Even if there is a spot open, any applicant needs to be performing at Level 1."

At that time, there was a new head of my client specialist group, Lee Spelman. She is now the head of U.S. Equity at J. P. Morgan Asset Management. I'm grateful that she is still a friend and mentor of mine today. We've known each other for over eighteen years. Lee told me, "You know what, Charisse? If you really want to get on the investment side, here's what I need from you. First, I need you to be performing at Level 1. Also, I need you to do what it takes to learn the craft of the investor role so that you can *prepare to perform* that role well. It will give you the credibility that you need." She added, "It's interesting that you said you want to move on the investment side, but you haven't taken the steps to get your CFA designation." The CFA designation takes three years on average to obtain, and it is the most recognized global investment designation in the field of asset management. Unless you have someone in your life who has the CFA, you probably have never heard of it.

As I explained in the previous chapter, the CFA designation stands for chartered financial analyst; this is a specialized designation within the larger business world, especially when compared to the MBA. It certifies that you have skills and expertise in quantitative analysis, economics, financial reporting, investment analysis, and portfolio management. Obtaining the CFA designation signals that you are an expert in understanding investments across a variety of asset classes: stocks, bonds, real estate, venture capital, and private equity. Back then, J. P. Morgan covered the registration fee, which is now $1,000 per level or $3,000 for all three levels for employees like me who wanted to take the test. You can tell how important the CFA designation is to the firm if it is willing to pay for its employees to get it. So Lee told me, "It's really a disconnect because if you really wanted to be on the investment side, you would have taken the steps to at least start that process."

That comment hit me like a ton of bricks, because she was absolutely right. If I wanted to learn the craft of investing, I had to take the actions that not only signaled that I was moving in the direction of being an investor, but also would legitimately give me the skill set to understand what investments are. That realization played a big part in my recognizing the power of learning the craft and spending the time to do so, even though it's hard and will probably take more time than you imagine.

It was the summer of 2003 when Lee gave me that feedback. I immediately started on the journey of registering for the CFA test. With the exception of Level 1, you can only take one level per year. It's a difficult and arduous exam, with an average pass rate between 40 and 50 percent across all three levels.[19] So I signed up to take Level 1 in December 2003, enrolled myself in a class, studied for four months, and ended up passing that first level. It was even harder because I did not have a background in finance. Rather, I had studied American studies and economics at Yale. That year was a grueling sacrifice because I spent ten to fifteen hours studying per week.

At the same time, I was also focused on doing my day job at a heightened level of excellence. We had half-year check-ins on our progress. By March 2004, I had indications that a spot would open up in the investment group that I wanted to get into. Lee, who had given me excellent advice about learning my craft and being patient, let me know that the spot was open, gave me feedback, said, "Hey,

Charisse, you're doing so well in this role. I don't want to hold you back. You just passed Level 1 of your CFA, and I see that you're also registered for Level 2 in the spring. So I want to put your name in the hat for this investment role."

Remember what I said about sponsors in Chapter 3? Lee became my effective sponsor. She advocated for me to move into that role. The person in charge of hiring for that spot was Jonathan Simon, who was a managing director, or "M.D.," at the time. An M.D. is pretty much the highest title that you can get at J. P. Morgan without being on the company's executive team. She suggested that he hire me for that open spot. While I was not in the conversation, I imagine that it went something like this from what I pieced together:

> *Jonathan: Why should we take Charisse? She doesn't have any experience in investing. We've also never taken someone this junior.*
>
> *Lee: Well, why not? She is committed to learning her craft. She has demonstrated a desire to do so, and she's excelling in her current role, which is no longer challenging her. You would do yourself a disservice if you did not hire her.*

Thanks to my performance, as well as Lee's faith in and sponsorship of me, I was hired on that team. You should know that I applied to two other investment roles during the six months prior , but I was not selected to join those teams. But the third time around, thankfully, I received the green light to move over to the investment side. After that move, I finished my CFA in 2006 and spent the next four years contributing to the investment team, where I had the opportunity to learn from other team members who had been investing for a long time.

One of the biggest reasons that I think people can perfect their craft is that they have the tutelage, or mentorship, of others. As I mentioned in Chapter 3, mentors invest time and energy into others. On-the-job mentors help mentees perfect their craft during the daily activities of performing that job, which can accelerate the mentee's own learning experience. My manager, Jonathan, became an incredible on-the-job mentor in helping me perfect my investing craft, as he would often break down complex theoretical concepts in an easy, practical way.

By the time I was twenty-eight, the U.S. stocks that I researched constituted roughly 18 percent of our $10 billion portfolio. Translation: as a twenty-eight-year-old I had responsibility for a significant portion of dollars in this particular fund. I would not have been able to do that had I not spent the time to learn the craft of investing from the CFA perspective, and absorbing and learning everything I could from the seasoned investors around me. Over time, I became confident in my decisions, confident in my research, and confident in picking stocks for the benefit of other institutional clients.

You should also know that I had the room to fail. I had that room because I was on a small team where I had the instruction of Jonathan, who was super-smart and super-committed to *his* craft, working above me. So I want to stress how valuable it can be for you to surround yourself with people who are incredibly tireless about their own craft. That way you understand what it takes to be not just good, but excellent.

As I reflect back on those four years, honing my craft was also shaped by having the time to focus. Back then, I could work long hours without strong pulls on my time from other people or welcome future responsibilities such as motherhood. When I was younger, the time I had for personal and professional development was one of my greatest assets.

While I could also argue that I'm more efficient with my time now, I had a different degree of freedom back then to wake up earlier and get to the office before everybody else. During those years, I was also usually the last one to leave. I left later because I needed to make up time, quite frankly, to give myself the best opportunity to increase my knowledge. Putting in the time helped me build my confidence, which still only happens when I invest the time to prepare and be better.

K. Anders Ericsson was known for saying that it takes approximately 10,000 hours (or ten years) to perfect your craft.[20] Malcolm Gladwell popularized that theory in his book *Outliers*.[21] Looking back, I know I put in at least

10,000 hours over the course of four years to learn how to invest in the U.S. stock market. The math doesn't lie: I worked ten-hour days, and even if I don't count weekends (which I did work sometimes), I clocked 10,400 hours over four years just working the business days.

I share my craft working story with you in the hope that it gives you insights into how I grew my confidence, which helped me excel as a stock picker. I want you to reflect on several strategies to work your craft.

Know Who Inspires You

At this point, I invite you to reflect on the question: "Who inspires you?" It can be someone from any walk of life. I've already shared how my sponsor, Lee Spelman, inspired me to pursue my craft while my manager, Jonathan Simon, inspired me to learn the craft of investing. I will always be grateful to both Lee and Jonathan for these inspirations. I'm sure you can think of at least one person you've personally crossed paths with who has inspired you in kind.

In reality, however, your inspiration may not come from a personal or professional connection. You may not have the fortune of getting inspiration from those in your orbit. For many people, inspiration comes from somebody you want to emulate whom you've never met but has qualities that you admire.

This brings me to one of my all-time-favorite performers who has never failed to inspire me:

Thank You, Tina Turner

Everyone has their unique gift to give to the world, and when you can marry that gift with seeing how that manifests itself into a vocation it is awe-inspiring. I trust that if you haven't yet found your gift, that something in this book will help you to discover it.

The elements of Tina Turner that inspire me are many. She is an extraordinary talent who inspires me through her song and dance abilities, her work ethic, her self-discipline, and self-care. Number one, however, is her passion for singing and dancing. It is very clear in how Tina performs that this is what she was made to do. She so genuinely shares her work with the world. When I look at Tina and her passion for her craft, it is also abundantly clear that she is someone who has always lived into her purpose.

The second thing about Tina that inspires me about the way she approached her craft is her work ethic. I read her autobiography *I, Tina: My Life Story*, and despite the challenges that she faced, including an incredible amount of emotional and physical abuse, it is clear that she worked very hard to elevate herself out of an unhealthy environment. It's also clear that she wanted badly to practice and perfect her craft to rise above all of the drama.

Tina's work ethic was also evidenced by her body. I mean, my goodness! She retired from live performances in 2009 at age 70, and if you ever had the pure pleasure of seeing her perform in person or on TV, you no doubt noticed her body looked more like someone around age thirty-five. She nurtured it along the way and took good care of herself.

She is also a very spiritual person. Although raised Baptist, in 1973 she became a follower of Nichiren Buddhism. She gives credit to the spiritual chant of "Nam Myoho Renge Kyo, Nam Myoho Renge Kyo" for helping her endure during difficult times and overcome them.

So in addition to her devoted work ethic, she made a commitment to taking care of her emotional and spiritual well-being. Tina has demonstrated a high level of self-care, which has inspired many like me. In order to perform at the top of my game and work my craft, I know that self-care is paramount for my success.

Tina richly exhibits a trifecta of passion, work ethic and self-care, which equates to self-love—something that everyone needs and deserves.

Accelerate Craft-Building by Reading and Listening

In addition to being inspired by others, one of the best ways to accelerate craft-building is to read about or listen to others who have mastered their craft. Now, are you having a "duh, Charisse" moment? Well, if have listened to one of my YouTube videos meant to accelerate your path toward building wealth, you should! As such, this is my strong attempt at reminding you how important *continued* reading and listening can be to accelerate your own craftsmanship.

Many people perfect their craft by hands-on experience because that's how they learn best. They are what's known as *kinesthetic learners*. Others perfect their craft by reading. That actually was the case with one of the most famous writers and artists whose words have left a legacy on many people: Maya Angelou. Maya, like many writers, talked about her avid consumption of books when she was alive, God bless her soul.

When I was starting with the investment group at J. P. Morgan, one of the first things that my manager, Jonathan, told me was, "Here is one book that changed my life and helped make me a good investor." The book was *The Money Masters* by John Train, about various financial investment wizards. I read it because I wanted to become an amazing investor like Jonathan, and it quickly became clear to me that Jonathan's investment philosophy was modeled after that of Warren Buffett, one of the greatest investors of all time.

So whatever your preferences are for how you want to perfect your craft, whether it's hands-on experience or reading your way to excellence, I encourage you to keep this in mind:

Someone else has done what you're doing, perhaps in a different way.

That's okay. Follow your own course because it is uniquely yours, but learn from the experience of others. I guarantee that one of your predecessors in your chosen craft has undoubtedly written something or spoken about it in podcasts, audiobooks, or YouTube along the way. And if no one has, I challenge you to write about your own craft-building journey.

So don't forget to access those written or audio sources because they can keep you focused, bolster your spirits, and give you added insight into what it takes to perfect that specific craft. By reading or hearing about the experiences of others, you can save yourself from making a number of mistakes.

You can save not only time but, I would add, a high degree of heartache, too. Heartache is simply part and parcel of anyone's journey on the road to mastering anything, but I do not want you to get weighed down by it. Instead, I want you to quickly overcome any obstacles or challenges that stand in your way.

Internalizing someone else's journey and their approach is bound to help you in ways that you probably couldn't have imagined.

Learn by Experience, a Master Teacher

There's no more effective way to learn than experience. At some point, you have to just do it. Reading and listening are only going to get you so far. But when it comes to *how you uniquely* perfect your craft, in a way that only you are meant to perfect it, there is no substitute for doing the darned thing! So to quote Nike's catchphrase, "Just do it!"

Once you start to work your craft and put forth the time and attention toward obtaining the skill set that allows your craft to really blossom, you have a baseline. You'll also then have some fundamental and foundational skill sets that are related to the craft that you are working toward. That'll probably get you 60 to 70 percent of the way there. But I implore you to understand that learning and working your craft never stops.

If you really want to perfect your craft, you have to commit to consistently fine-tune and build on your foundational skills so that you move the needle from that 60 to 70 to 80 to 90 percent, and then ultimately 100 percent.

One of the professional challenges I experienced, after creating a baseline of foundational investing skills, was leaving J. P. Morgan right when the stock market crashed, in the summer of 2008. I left for business school, to get a broader business skill set and expand my network. That was absolutely the right choice to make in my own journey, because I knew I had a calling in my life to do something different outside the walls of J. P. Morgan and the world of professional stock investing.

Everyone knows what happened in fall 2008, the pinnacle of the Great Recession, when the financial markets and major institutions like Lehman Brothers came crashing down with ferocious speed. I had been investing on behalf of clients at the start of the Great Recession in late 2007 through May 2008, when I left for business school.

Trust me, I was incredibly grateful to not have to stomach the stock market meltdown.

On the flipside, I missed professionally investing through a huge downturn, which would have perfected my craft in new ways. When a new normal is created due to unpredictable circumstances, there is a tremendous opportunity for growth and new learning. Environments change. Times change. It's in these changing times that you can perfect your craft. While I was not investing professionally at this time, I did continue investing in my personal brokerage account to hone my craft.

My coworkers who remained at J. P. Morgan during the Great Recession were able to take that professional experience and apply it to other major stock market downturns, like the one we faced with the onset of COVID-19 in January 2020 and the collapse in the first months of the year. Even though the 2020 stock market is still a different environment, my former colleagues were able to rely on the muscles that they had built in the previous environment. They were better prepared to cope and maneuver for their clients given their 2008 experience. Many of them channeled learnings from the Great Recession, and by having experienced the 2008 debacle firsthand, they built their craft.

New environments and new seasons will bring the opportunity to fine-tune your craft and perfect it. While it's often painful as you go through these refining moments, you will gain valuable new tools and the ability to handle the pressures that come with making your craft what it is.

When I say, "Work your craft," I believe you'll find that by doing so, you will establish a foundation of skills to build on. These have been especially important to my journey, and I think at some point there's a starting point and a path to growth in skill for everybody.

Expect Setbacks in Order to Better Overcome Them

Part of working your craft also involves experiencing setbacks. I know this is hard to hear, easier said than done. I've experienced many setbacks, and I know that everyone does at one point or another. I want to push you further and challenge you to develop a healthy habit: to expect and be ready for setbacks.

A quick flashback from my own experience might help illustrate this. As I mentioned, the pass rate for the CFA exams overall is 40 to 50 percent. On my way to getting my CFA designation, in 2004 I failed Level 2. The pass rate that year was 32 percent. Think about that for a moment. Almost 7 out of 10 people failed the Level 2 test that year, and I was one of them. Now, that 32 percent pass rate is the lowest Level 2 pass rate in the history of the CFA exam from 1963 to 2019. I then went on to pass Level 2 in 2005 and Level 3 in 2006. I failed that 2004 test, and it was an incredible blow to my confidence and to all of the work that I put in.

After all, it took six months to study for each level, which meant six months of limiting my social activities with family and friends, while at the same time studying for roughly ten to fifteen hours a week. Simultaneously, I was transitioning into that new investor role at J. P. Morgan, which meant that I had to put in extra time to learn and execute that job properly. It also took six months of praying and asking God to give me the strength. Through all of that, I still failed Level 2. I remember getting the results in the mail and being so disheartened because I had worked so hard.

There are many, many people who fail at many things. What's important is knowing that it's not about whether you fail, but more importantly, whether you keep going. How are you going to respond in the face of failure? If you are determined like I was, ultimately you must keep your eye on the prize, as the saying goes, and understand that failure is just a stepping stone toward your goal and a building block toward your resiliency.

In my case, I had to remember what many of my colleagues told me before I even took the test: "expect to fail *at least* one level. It's going to happen." You see, most people do fail at least one level of the CFA. Even though I heard this before I took the test, I believed that I was going to be an exception to failure, which is flawed thinking. I was overconfident, and so the setback was even harder to absorb.

I slowly gave myself permission to expect a setback. It took me a long time—many months—to learn this lesson. I don't want you to wallow in your setbacks. If you anticipate the setbacks, you can shorten the amount of time that you hold onto the disappointment of them. Here, you can set yourself free from the embarrassment and shame that often accompanies them.

And I highly recommend making your disappointment time extremely short. Otherwise, the disappoint-ment will play with your psyche and negatively affect your confidence. When you anticipate setbacks, the interim roadblocks seem normal and part of the journey, rather than huge and horrible barriers. Setbacks will be a factor in just about any vocation. As such, do not define yourself by the setback, but rather by what you accomplish along your entire journey.

Finally, I want you to not only celebrate the successes along your journey, but also be thankful for what you learn from your setbacks and disappointments. For me, I remember the day I went back into the office after taking the Level 2 exam. On my floor, the two other people who took the test were among the 30 percent who passed. I gave them an outward congratulatory smile as I inwardly berated myself for failing.

I literally wanted to hide under my desk so that I could be invisible to my colleagues. I felt ashamed. I felt less than. What I eventually reminded myself of was this: 1) my journey is my own, and 2) I need not compare myself to others and the timeline of their journey. My colleagues who passed were not dealing with my circumstances. For instance, they were not transitioning to a new investor role. Also, they both had a background in finance. So they had a different starting point than I did, with my background in economics and American studies.

You never know where other people are in their own skill and craft-building journey. So comparing yourself to someone else without knowing their full story can create a false bar for you to meet if you're using their measuring stick and their timeline against your own.

I strongly encourage you to expect setbacks to come. And when they do, respond in a way that keeps you running your race toward the finish line. Yes, you might be in a study group and yes, you might try and work your craft with other people, but ultimately, you still must run your own race. Commit to yourself that your craft journey is yours alone. You deserve this freedom from *comparisonitis* and heartache. En route, you can work your craft, which will help you obtain your wealth.

Develop Personal Disciplines

For your own Wealthy Girl craft-building journey, I encourage you to see that it is very much a journey of the heart, filled with nuances. You can definitely find ways to move from thinking, "How on earth do I go from 'I don't ever see myself other than where I'm at right now,' to 'Oh, my gosh! Life is ever-expanding. I see possibilities and I am creating the mindset and the heartset to make it work.'"

I did it, and so will you!

My journey has been very personal, and I set up a number of disciplines so that I could keep moving toward the reward of perfecting my craft, which is a key component of intangible wealth. My journey to get my CFA forced me to develop some personal disciplines along the way. First, I set aside time every week to pray and go to church. I made a promise to myself that, "Yes, I am going to be studying and working my craft in order to develop a craft around investment. But I'm also going to allow myself to do what I need to do in order to feed my soul."

Feeding my soul meant that Sunday was "no investments" and "no craft" day. For that one day, I decided not to do any work or any studying because I needed to restore myself. That was because from Monday through Saturday, it took all of my energy to try and work my craft. My personal discipline of restoration occurred through the soul-giving act of being in church and praying. Spiritual restoration, however you define it for yourself, can be a powerful discipline for you as well.

The second discipline I developed during my journey to develop my craft was intentional focus. I intentionally set apart time weekly to work on my craft. Part of my intentionality meant making sure that I communicated what I was doing to the other people in my life who loved me: my friends and family. I said something of this effect to many of them: "I need time to focus on studying for my test. It's not that I don't care, but the focus required for me to pass this test demands my attention. I love you and I will call you back, but it may not be immediately." Like me, you may have to give up things that normally might be part of your life so you can focus on developing your craft. By communicating your intentions to others, you can set up boundaries that allow you to focus while minimizing potential damage to your relationships. Your true friends will be there on the other side of any intentional time focus to celebrate with you. If your "friend" is annoyed by your attempt to focus on your craft, I encourage you to question the basis of that friendship.

The personal disciplines of both spiritual restoration and intentional focus into achieving your goals are critically important. In fact, the spiritual restoration discipline helps enable my intentional focus discipline. These personal disciplines are also standalone contributors to building intangible wealth in your life. You can apply these personal disciplines not only to working your craft, but also to *anything* important in your life.

Focusing on yourself doesn't mean that you're selfish, even though the world will try and tell you that it is. If you don't invest in you, how can you expect others to believe in you or get the results you want? Focusing on yourself means going after the purpose that God has given you, and living a purposeful life is one of the biggest intangible wealth creators you can ever have.

Chapter Takeaways

It may seem simple, but you can only work your craft if you know what your craft is. Many people fail to figure out what their craft truly is, let alone how to work it. That won't be you.

So, I leave you with these important questions:

- *What is your craft?*
- *What's stopping you from working your craft?*
- *What setbacks should you expect as you continue to work your craft?*
- *How can you use your personal disciplines to work your craft moving forward?*

Onward you go!

Step 3: Develop an Investor Mindset

I F YOU'RE GOING TO be a Wealthy Girl, developing an investor mindset is an absolute must. I know what you're thinking: "I'm not good at math," or "I'm not good at managing my finances." Stop these thoughts, as that line of thinking reflects Myth 4, "I don't have the skill set to build wealth," which we discussed in Chapter 2.

You *can* develop an investor mindset. It takes believing in the life you want, action, and confidence.

One person who developed an investor mindset is my mother. Her story is impressive because she has created a life of investment across the tangible and intangible aspects of wealth.

To understand her mindset, you must understand my mother's background. My mother, Barbara Ann Shine Conanan, is the oldest child of Naomi Shine, my Grandma Shine, who I described in Chapter 1. As with many firstborn children, Barbara has carried the responsibility to care for and be a positive example for her siblings. Her mother always told her, "Barbara, whatever you do, your siblings will follow." Investors show with their actions. My grandmother instilled in my mother the importance of leading by example.

Growing up in Harlem during the 1950s, my mother was shaped by her environment. She knew early on that education was her ticket to the life she dreamed. As I mentioned in Chapter 1, my Grandma Shine graduated valedictorian of her high school, but her parents lacked the money to send her to college. Thus, Grandma Shine poured all of her formal educational desires into her children, starting with my mom. My mother was the first in her family to attend college, staying local and attending Bronx Community College. She invested her time and talent to pursue nursing. She loved the idea of caring for others, and to this day "loves those white uniforms."

When my mother graduated from nursing school, she went on to Lehman College, where she met my father, who charmed her with his good looks and intelligence, Black and Filipino swag, and his romantic antics. She immediately invested in this relationship; she dropped the guy she was dating and put all her attention on my dad after a few dates. I call her a 1970s-style "playa," but I'm proud of her choice in my dad, and I'm the blessed beneficiary of their sizzling relationship.

They married at age twenty-three and had my brother Clayton and then me before they turned thirty. One year after she had me, my mother decided to make another investment—this time in her career, which would build on her nursing experience. She dedicated the next thirty-six years of her life providing healthcare services to homeless populations in New York City. Come on! Who stays in the same career for more than thirty years these days?

In practical terms, this meant that she stopped the daily grind of nursing and transitioned into administering health care to homeless persons on behalf of St. Vincent's Hospital in New York City. There, she shaped the Community Medicine program, the first of its kind in the U.S. Today, there are 300 programs across the nation modeled after that original program, which revolves around a simple idea: providing holistic healthcare to homeless populations in a community setting. They execute on the program by having hospital staff—doctors, nurses, psychiatrists, social workers, outreach workers, administrators—go into homeless shelters in and around New York and provide healthcare services.

Not only was Community Medicine the first of its kind, but my mother was spearheading efforts during the rise of the AIDS epidemic, which especially ravaged homeless populations. My mother and her boss, Philip Brickner, wrote two books, *Healthcare for the Homeless* and *Under the Safety Net: The Health and Social Welfare of the Homeless in the United States*, which provide detailed glimpses of my mother's work. I continue to uncover new learnings from these books to this day. As I watched her through the years in that career, which came to a graceful end when she retired in 2017, I knew that she was living into her life's purpose. The decisions she made over that thirty-six-year span are rooted in a willingness to invest in herself, her children, her husband, and her community.

Along the way, my mother always believed in having tangible wealth, in addition to the intangible ways in which she showed up as a mother to me. For example, when I got accepted to attend Yale, she didn't have as much money saved for me to attend college as she initially wanted. When I was a toddler, she and my dad had invested their money with a financial advisor for my college education. During the late 1980s, however, the stock market crashed. Their portfolio was not diversified, and my parents lost nearly all of my college savings. I cringe every time my mom tells me this story! I mean, my parents tried to do all the right things, and then it all came crashing down.

Sadly, that financial advisor had not invested their portfolio wisely. My mom was outraged when she discovered they didn't have as much as they had planned for my brother's and my college funds. This reality spurred her to learn about investing, specifically in stocks, for herself. She said to me, "I might as well. I can do bad all by myself." While my mom has used financial advisors since that bad experience, she is now empowered and educated on how to utilize them effectively.

She subsequently committed herself to educating herself on investments. About two months before I left for college, my mom called her stockbroker to purchase Dell computers stock. At the time, it seemed like everyone had a Dell computer, including my mom. She wanted to take advantage of what she saw around her and earn a little extra money to help pay for my education. Instead of only being a consumer of Dell products, she became an investor in Dell stock.

At the time, I had no idea how investing worked. She explained that you could own part of a company through buying stock, and if the company did well, you would do well, too. So I asked her if I could also buy some Dell stock, and she bought me about $2,500 worth before I left for Yale. Dell stock was trading around $16 per share.

I headed off to college, forgetting all about that Dell stock. Fast forward to four-and-a-half years later, Mom sent me her brokerage statement, and it showed that my Dell stock had turned into almost $4,400 because its stock price reached $28.30 in November 2002, a few months after I graduated. I couldn't believe it. My $2,500 had almost doubled. I loved the fact that I had extra money, especially since that was my very first experience with stocks. I sold my Dell stock and used those profits to pay down some of my student loan debt.

As I said, my mother is not a financial person by profession: she's a healthcare professional. But she pays attention to what is happening around her as a consumer, and thus she has incredible insight because she's focused on connecting daily living to investing. Mom also acts quickly on her wisdom, as she did during the COVID-19 era by buying Zoom stock in early March when the stock was at $125 per share. By late September 2020, the stock was trading at over $500 per share.

Between the time I went to college and 2020, my mother has been part of stock investing clubs, signed up for investing classes, and read a ton of books like this one. She has generated ample returns for her family due to her investing activities. You too can be like my mother: learning from past mistakes to reach your goals, learning investing skills, taking action toward your goals, and making money.

When investing in stocks or other asset classes, many people struggle to stay focused and use available information to their advantage. I share my mother's story with you to highlight certain attributes that made her successful. I got some of that investor DNA from her to develop my investor mindset, and here's all you need to do in order to develop an investor mindset for yourself.

Become the CEO of Your Wealth

Having an investor mindset starts on the inside. When you tell yourself that you're going to be CEO of your wealth, you then assume the chief executive officer's role in the tangible and intangible aspects of your wealth. When you're the CEO of your wealth, you treat your wealth as a business, and you are in charge of making your wealth goals a reality.

Three key attributes that can help you assume the position of CEO of your wealth are:

Vision. You must become the visionary. Here you create the vision for what you need your wealth to look like, and what you need your life to look like. In doing so, you stay focused on the vision that becomes the guiding light for where you spend your precious money, resources, and time. Great CEOs have great vision and make decisions every day based on their vision. They also stay focused, muting out the distractions that will surely come along.

Action orientation. You must take action on your own or find help. It's hard to take action without having a philosophy around wealth creation. Your philosophy should be based on your values, including how you prioritize allocating your money and time. In essence, how are you going to take action? When your approach links to your values, then it becomes much easier to take action. And you're going to move in an active way such that you stay in front of what you want to achieve and how you want to achieve it.

Taking action means staying on the offensive, not the defensive, looking to seize opportunity because you've prepared accordingly.

Confidence. Building confidence will come from surrounding yourself with an A-Team, or people who can assist you with executing on your vision. Your A-Team should include an excellent financial advisor (or the COO of your wealth) or an informal peer group that we've talked about in Chapter 4. Moreover, confidence comes with having helpful tools and products, or the infrastructure, to effectively execute on your wealth goals.

Even when you make mistakes, you'll need the confidence to learn from those mistakes and ensure that they don't repeat themselves. As I reflect on my mom and the mistakes that she made in picking a bad financial advisor, she didn't let that hold her back from growing. She used that experience to gain the confidence she needed as she educated herself on investing after that.

To recap, being visionary, action-oriented, and confident are attributes you want exercise as the CEO of your wealth so that you ultimately gain that investor mindset.

The Visionary at Work

Let's talk more about being a visionary. Here, your dreams must come first. First you have to identify what your dreams are. Dream identification seems like an easy task, right? Sadly, I think that as we get older, it becomes more and more difficult to dream about what you want your life to be, especially those big dreams. The routines of life settle in, including the monotony of paying bills, going to work, or taking care of others. We forget to dream again, like when we were kids.

One way to bring your dreams to life is to create a vision board. Vision boards can come in the form of pictures you take and stick on a board or cut-outs from magazines glued to a piece of paper. The important thing about a vision board is that it reflects what you want in your life, or your dreams' visual manifestation.

I created my vision board with a group of ten girlfriends right after the new year in 2018. I still have this vision board, which I often looked for inspiration as I sometimes wrote this book at five a.m. If you were to visit me and take a look at it, you'd see pictures of slogans that read "Be the Boss," "I'm positive about my future. And the strategy to get there," "Are you wasting time, energy, money?" as well as pictures of a family with children. There's also an image of a woman dancing with a massive smile on her face and arms up in the air a house, and a picture of a microphone.

I often get goosebumps when I look at this vision board. By the end of that year, I had purchased a new home, begun to prepare for my first child to arrive, and started to use my microphone (which had been sitting in an unopened gift box for two years) to record videos for my Charisse Says YouTube videos. My vision board helped me visualize my dreams and invest in the daily actions to make them a reality. I want you to visualize your dreams too.

And you must carve out at least a small amount of time to visualize your dreams every day. I am a fan of doing the deep work necessary to help you achieve your dreams. The term "deep work" was made popular by blogger, professor, and author Cal Newport, in *Deep Work: Rules for Focused Success in a Distracted World.*[22] His simple four steps—work deeply, embrace boredom, quit social media, drain the shallow—provide a blueprint for focus.

These steps can help you focus on what's most important in your life and career without getting distracted and bogged down by the "information overload" of emails, social media, and text notifications that ping you every moment. For instance, I've turned off the notification button on my phone at specific periods of the day when I want to focus on my writing, and I am no longer interrupted by that very annoying ping of my phone. I swear that my brain is incredibly happy since it has grown accustomed to long stretches of quiet.

In order to invest in yourself and your dreams first, you've got to make time and space to allow them to come to fruition so you can obtain the wealth you desire, every single day. It's a daily journey, and you might be saying, "Well, but Charisse, it's hard to make that time and space every day." I hear you, but I want you to remember what we talked about the myth of "I do not have the skill set" back in Chapter 2.

You can learn how to focus by practicing every single day. You can set aside time on a consistent basis to channel your energy into the things you want to accomplish. You'll discover that this is an incredibly effective roadmap to the fruition of your dreams, and internalizing your CEO of wealth status.

Putting your dreams first is not about being selfish, because selfishness implies a lack of consideration for others. That's not what I'm talking about. What I'm recommending is that you focus on putting yourself first. This means learning that you are considering your own well-being first and foremost, and if you do that right, you can be there for others. It might not be as obvious as it sounds, but trust me: after trying to put others before myself for many years, I can tell you that does not work.

Interestingly enough, our male counterparts seem to have an easier time with allocating time for themselves. I look at my husband, who prioritizes his time for himself with absolutely no problem at all. This may be due to some old-school conditioning that has been prevalent for centuries, where women were expected, and in some cases demanded, to take a backseat to their husband, male boss, or other men in their lives.[23] I admit, focusing on yourself is hard, especially if you are like me, and care about your career and your household.

In the twenty-first century, women have evolved culturally to not just be caretakers, but in many cases, to also be breadwinners.

Simultaneously, the number of stay-at-home dads has risen significantly. Since 2010, the number of stay-at-home dads has doubled to 1.4 million.[24] That said, a friend brought up an interesting question last year. She asked,

"Don't you feel that you still do the brunt of household chores and childcare?" While we're admittedly grateful that a lot more men help out around the house these days, national studies have shown that married mothers in the U.S. increased their primary childcare hours from 10.6 in 1965 to 12.6 in 2000, while at the same time married fathers increased their hours from 2.6 to 6.5. Married mothers have dealt with more intensive parenting at the same time that they have experienced higher demands on their careers.[25] While the quantifiable data is scant on these trends over the last twenty years, the lived experiences and stories of many women affirm the reality of higher demands on their time.

So, how do we *stay* a visionary?

Taking steps in that direction requires intentionally focusing on you and forgiving yourself when you don't always get it right. But in the end, if you can get in the habit of taking care of yourself first, similarly to how we covered perfecting your craft, then you will be able to internalize that investor mindset that starts with you. It's incredibly important.

As you go on your journey to put yourself first and execute on your ideas, there may be people around you, and it could even be your partner or spouse, family members or friends, who will look at you with a side-eye and think that you are not prioritizing the right things. Regardless of the naysayers, you must keep it moving.

Taking Action

Once you've made time to work on your vision, you must take action. Great investors are on the offensive, not the defensive, when it comes to building wealth. They are prepared to seize opportunity when it presents itself. When you want to build tangible wealth, being on the offensive means that you're aggressively focused on both asset building *and* debt paydown. One of your overarching goals should be to have more assets than debt, and thus build your tangible wealth levels.

Now, you might be saying, "Well, Charisse, I do have a lot of debt and it hamstrings me from focusing on saving and investing." You might need to do some work to get your debt under control. However, that does not exclude you from thinking about your wealth from an asset perspective, and from taking an offensive way of thinking about your money. You can have an asset-building approach to your money by using an action-oriented allocation strategy. After spending many hundreds of hours speaking with individuals about investing, I developed a proprietary allocation strategy called the "SIPPin' & Livin'" strategy. I am now sharing this strategy with you. I've taught this strategy to individuals and families over many years through online classes and workshops. SIPPin' & Livin' lets you to put all your money that you have coming in, or your income, in one of two categories.

Let me break it down for you. SIPPin' is:

- Saving
- Investing
- Protecting
- Paying down

And Living is everything else: housing expenses, childcare, transportation, groceries—everything you spend money on to live your life. We'll go through more of the details in just a minute.

I hate the word budget because it feels so constraining to me. You've heard it all before: "Budget your money so you don't spend it all. Stick to your budget."

The problem is, the exercise of creating a budget is daunting, unwelcome, and tiring, particularly if you don't have a lot of money. If that's the case, why budget? The only people who feel good about a budget are those who can stick to it, and most of us can't stick to it. But if you do, good for you and I still want you to consider my SIPPin' & Livin' allocation strategy.

An allocation strategy can help you accelerate your wealth goals and will help you be more on the offensive with your tangible money. I prefer the word *allocation* as opposed to budgeting. When you allocate your money, you're empowered because you direct where your money goes. Since you want to assume the position of CEO of your wealth that we talked about earlier in the chapter, you hold the power of figuring out how to allocate your precious resources.

In order to execute on the SIPPin' & Livin' strategy, you must have some income to allocate. Gross income is money you have coming in from any source (working, income from investments in your portfolio, and so on) on a recurring basis, whether daily, weekly, biweekly, bimonthly, or monthly. One typical form of gross income is salary, the amount of money your employer pays you before any money (such as taxes or retirement account contributions) is taken out. If you are not a salaried employee, but you make income on an hourly basis, this strategy will fit you too.

Other advisors and strategists will tell you to start with your "take-home" income (what actually hits your bank account after taxes and the like are taken out), but this misses a huge opportunity for you to create a holistic allocation and make informed choices. Using your gross income number offers more flexibility because so many of the things that are taken out before your gross income (like taxes, health insurance premiums, retirement contributions, and so on) are adjustable. Most people forget that they have already put aside money for investment in their 401k accounts, so they forget to include these when creating their allocations—which defeats the purpose and fails to credit them with accomplishing their investing goals.

Also, more and more people have some form of income from independent contracting and entrepreneurship, thus the gross income number is even more relevant. We will talk about the importance of entrepreneurship and starting a business in Chapter 7, but for now, know that you can consider income from your business in the income bucket.

If you have two or more jobs, you should combine all of the gross incomes into one gross income number to provide a complete picture of all of your money sources. Don't include one-time sources of income such as bonuses, gifts, and tax refunds in this gross income number on a recurring basis. Including your one-time income sources as part of your gross income can create a false sense of security because these sources are not recurring. Finally, you might have passive income coming into your bank account on a consistent basis. I'm a big fan of passive income. As opposed to ordinary earned income and portfolio income, those who have a high financial IQ focus on creating passive income, which tends to flow from entities like royalties, business distributions, and yes, real estate.

The way that it works is that you commit to allocating all of your gross income, first toward the SIPPin' categories, and then you keep living your life and allocate income toward the Living categories.

Let's SIPP First

Let's start with the SIPPin' portion: saving, investing, protecting, and paying down. These are all terms that you are probably familiar with, but I will define them to be sure that we are on the same page.

Saving. Saving means putting money aside in a separate savings account that is used for emergencies and things you want to buy (such as a new TV) or experiences you want to have (like visiting China to learn about the culture, attending an out-of-town wedding, or undergoing a health procedure not covered by your insurance) within the next twenty-four months. I suggest that you save up for what you want in an account that is separate from your normal checking account. By putting money in a separate savings account, we can help ourselves to control our temptations. As hard as it may be to use a separate account initially, you will benefit in both the short term and long term.

The point most people forget about savings is that your savings are intended to be used at some point. So, you will have to replenish them after you've made a purchase or used the money for some other purpose.

Investing. Investing means putting money aside in separate investment accounts which can be used for mid-term (three to five years away) and long-term (more than five years in the future) goals such as a child's education, retirement, or a stash for future generations. With investing, your goal should be to generate a positive return on the initial money that you put in. The major investing asset classes that you can expect a positive return from over time are stocks, bonds, real estate, venture capital (start-ups and small businesses), and private equity (companies held privately).

Now, just because you *expect* a positive return doesn't mean that you'll actually achieve it. In some cases, your investments might lose money like those that I shared about my mom at the beginning of the chapter. When you invest, you risk losing money too. So when we talk about the investing portion of SIPPin' & Livin', make sure that you can do a little bit of everything. And I know that sounds like, "Well, Charisse, if I'm investing in the stock market through my retirement account, I can't also do real estate and I can't do _____ (you fill in the blank with your objection)." Or, perhaps it's also about investing in somebody else's business.

I'm not saying that you have to do it all at once, but I am saying that diversification matters. Adhering to the old adage of not putting all your eggs in one basket stands the test of time, because if that basket breaks, it'll be a problem. To this end spread out your investable assets across a variety of investment opportunities such as real estate and stocks and bonds so that you can reap the benefits of diversification. If one of your investments starts doing well you have a buffer if another does not perform. I know it sounds counterintuitive because, ideally, you want all of your investments to do well at the same time. But that's not how these asset classes work. They're uncorrelated, meaning they don't move in the same direction at the same time. That's why diversification is a really good thing. If something goes wrong in one place, you have cushions somewhere else. Please just remember that commitment to investing in diverse asset classes is extremely important.

Protecting. Protecting involves buying a financial product that will protect you if something bad, small or large, happens in the future. These financial products typically come in the form of insurance (health, life, car, renter's, disability, etc.) and contribute positively to your overall health and prevent you from losing money. Your biggest insurance cost will most likely be health insurance, which will grow in importance over the next several years as employers shift more costs to employees and as individuals shop for their own insurance as a result of the Affordable Care Act.

Paydown. Paying down involves paying off your interest-bearing balances to any institutions to which you owe money. You are typically charged interest (the extra cost of owing money to an institution or person) when you do not pay for a good or service in full. You pay interest when you borrow money from someone else in order to pay for a good or service, or when you do not pay for something in full within a specified time period, usually a month.

Examples of outstanding interest-bearing debts are credit card balances that are not paid in full by the cards' due dates, student loan balances, car loan balances, and even money you have borrowed from a friend who charged you an extra lending fee. I have purposely not included mortgages (loans you get when you purchase a house but cannot pay for it in full right away).

Because a mortgage represents the cost of your ongoing housing expense, I have instead included it in the housing bucket in the Livin' strategy, which I'll discuss later. You can choose to rent or buy housing, but the fact remains that housing is a need, so it should be considered separately, regardless of how you finance that decision.

Also, I have excluded credit card balances that are paid off every month because you are not charged interest on those balances. If you pay off your credit card balance every month, do not count the balance as part of your paying down category, as this action is part of Livin'— stuff you do to live your life. Similarly, if you open a twelvemonth, o percent APR credit card from Home Depot, do not count this as part of your paying down bucket for the first twelve months because there is no interest attached to this balance. This card would fall under the Livin' strategy, as you will see later.

Now, Get to the Livin'

The Living part of SIPPin' & Livin' encompasses everything you need to live, utilizing your gross income to obtain all the things you need and want to spend money on. For me, for example, reducing stress is a need, but how I spend money to do so is arbitrary. For each person, needs and wants are different, so I have created a simple category scheme that includes basic needs common to almost everyone and allows you the freedom to define needs for yourself.

I break down all of these Livin' activities into just a few categories because you only need a few to create and stick to your allocation. Often, my clients get overwhelmed by all of the categories they can split their money into, but I've found that by minimizing the number of expense categories, I can save people lots of headaches and dollars. There are four Livin' categories: income taxes, giving, housing, and everything else. At the end of the chapter, I provide an easy table to illustrate each category.

Income taxes. The amount paid in taxes is defined here as the dollar amount your job sets aside (withholds) from your check during each pay period. Remember, federal and state governments mandate that employers withhold taxes from your check because Uncle Sam does not trust you to pay taxes on your own. When you file your tax return in April, you are reconciling with the government: Did your employer take out too much or too little in taxes? Do you owe the IRS more money, or does the IRS owe you money (a tax refund)?

If you're an independent contractor, the tax amount represents the amount you pay directly to the federal and state government every quarter.

Unfortunately, Uncle Sam wants a lot of our money to do stuff. I do not mind paying taxes, but I do not want to pay an amount that leaves me speechless or give the government more than its fair share of my earnings. If you earn more than $600 in a calendar year, you must pay taxes.

Giving. Giving captures the donations you make to non-profit organizations that you support financially. A tithe is a specific kind of giving set aside for a church or religious organization. In the Christian community, for example, the requested tithe is 10 percent of your annual earnings. While there is much debate as to whether 10 percent should be taken from gross or net income, we will assume that all tithes are taken from your gross income. If giving to charitable organizations does not apply to you, you can remove this from your allocation.

Housing. Housing refers to the recurring amount set aside to live indoors. Examples of recurring housing expenses are rent paid to a landlord, a mortgage paid to a financial institution, housing taxes, and mortgage insurance. Notice that I included mortgage insurance under the housing category instead of the protection category. Many people pay their home insurance and taxes with their mortgage; thus, pragmatically, it makes no sense to separate them. But feel free to separate them out if you prefer. The truth of the matter is that you should not own or even rent a home without home or renter's insurance, so wherever you put it, this expense should go somewhere. Also, the cost is so small that it will have a muted effect on your overall allocation.

Everything else. The "everything else" category refers to exactly what the name implies: everything else. Whether you buy food at the grocery store or in a nice restaurant, you've got to eat, so you will spend money on food. I do not want you to get caught like a deer in headlights creating subcategories like childcare, groceries, entertainment, restaurants, and food on trips. One month you may eat out a lot, and the next month you may not, so it is very important to keep this category broad to capture everything.

If you're fortunate enough to have your meals paid for, as is the case with many consultants or investment bankers, then kudos to you; your everything else category will most likely be lower than normal. Other examples include goods for the house, personal items such as deodorant and getting your hair and nails professionally styled. The key is that this category captures what is not included in the other four Living categories or the four SIPPin' categories.

So what does this SIPPin' & Livin' categorization scheme look like in practice? Your specific SIPPin' & Livin' strategy will be contingent on the amount of income coming in because of the so-called wealth effect—people with more income tend to have the capacity to save more and invest more.

In my classes that I've taught online, the SIPPin' & Livin' strategy works across the majority of professional income levels. For instance, whether your household makes $30,000, $75,000, or over $150,000, you can apply the SIPPin' & Livin' strategy. If you make significantly less than $30,000 the SIPPin' & Livin' strategy does not work so well, and your personal situation will require a set of strategies that are beyond the scope of this book.

For example, if you make $75,000, I suggest you put approximately 7 percent, or $5,250, of your gross income into savings, and 13 percent, or $9,750, into investments. Now, my recommendation is a guideline and you can dial up or down based on your comfort level, your goals, and consultation with your financial advisor. Also, if you have outstanding debt balances that have a high interest rate debt (e.g., a credit card balance of $3,000 with an annual interest rate of 20 percent on that balance), you will want to allocate some of your income to paying off high-interest rate debt than investing in stocks, for example.

One successful trade-off strategy that I've employed for myself, and for clients, is to allocate some of your money toward the highest rate, whether it's paying down debt or investing. So, if the credit card company is charging you 20 percent and you expect the U.S. stock market to return 7 percent (which is the average return of U.S. stocks over the long-term), then you will want to ensure that a portion of your money goes toward paying down that credit card debt quickly because it's a higher interest rate relative to the stock investment.

I know, it sounds counterintuitive because you are paying down a debt, but if you don't pay down any portion of that debt, you will be charged 20 percent and if you took that same money and put it in stocks and it returned

7 percent, you would still need to eventually pay more money on the debt. In the chapter takeaway below, I provide a full table of suggested guidelines of the percentages that you can allocate for each SIPPin' & Livin' category at different annual income levels from $30,000 to $200,000 (for a single person).

To bring SIPPin' & Livin' to life with an example, one of the places that you can invest is real estate. And I know you've heard, "Invest in real estate! Invest in real estate! It's a great way to make money!" Over and over again, right? Well, I have found this to be true, but the beauty of this comes into play when you can actually generate passive income from it. So real estate is a way for you to have an asset-producing investment in order to have money go into your pocket.

I'm far from the first person to talk about real estate. But I want to illustrate how real estate investing can generate passive income for you and thus provide more opportunity to move toward your wealth goals. Passive income strategies were made popular by financial guru Robert Kiyosaki in the late 1990s in *Rich Dad, Poor Dad*.[26] His business and some of his advice have come under pretty severe scrutiny in recent years, but I draw on his passive income philosophy because it changed the way I think about real estate.

Most importantly, Kiyosaki encourages us to know what kind of income you're working for and to focus on passive income.[27] When you receive rent from property that you own, you receive passive income. Passive income flows to you regardless of whether you're working or not and allows you to trade fewer hours for dollars. Passive income is the lowest-taxed form of income and has numerous tax benefits. Therefore, it's one of the most simple and effective means of creating tangible wealth.

I have personally used the SIPPin' & Livin' strategy in my own life throughout adulthood when I made less money and when I made more money. Several months before I moved from New York to Chicago to start business school at the University of Chicago Booth School of Business, I contemplated what to do with the $50,000 I had saved up over five years from 2003 to 2008. Basically, I saved $10,000 per year (on average) because of my SIPPin' & Livin' approach. My savings stash didn't just happen overnight.

Now, it helped tremendously that I got a full academic scholarship to attend Chicago Booth and thus didn't have to tap my savings for school tuition. And I didn't want to put that $50,000 in the stock market because I already had a decent stash of money in my 401k retirement account, and I wanted to diversify my assets. Real estate investing seemed like a good alternative.

So, at age twenty-eight, I decided to buy real estate property with that $50,000 in Hyde Park, Chicago, and close enough to business school. In May 2008, before the height of the Great Recession and a clamp-down on credit, I bought a two-bedroom, two-bath condo using my savings for a down payment on the house and getting a mortgage for the rest. I also gave myself a time horizon by planning to hold onto the condo for at least five years, and for at least two of those years, renting out the second bedroom while I went to school, to have somebody help pay for my mortgage. That real estate investment enabled me to generate passive income to the tune of $800 a month, which I applied to my expenses.

Powerful, right? I also said to myself that if I decided to move away from Chicago, I would still hold the condo for a few years in the hope of getting some appreciation in its value. My success in making that real estate investment was two-fold. First, I was prepared financially with my credit score and down payment to secure a mortgage on the house. Second, I was mentally prepared to seize the investing opportunity. As you build tangible wealth, your ability to seize opportunities will accelerate based on financial and emotional preparation. It's possible!

The way it actually worked out was that I stayed in Chicago after school, and thus continued to rent my condo to roommates for three years, then lived alone for two years; and then my husband moved in with me in 2013. I was able to not only decrease my housing expense, but also have this additional income stream while I went to school because of the investment I made when I needed additional income coming in.

Fast forward to 2018 and we moved out of that condo because we wanted a place with more space and a fresh start, especially given our goals to have children. We did so because we employed a joint SIPPin' & Livin' strategy, saving money for a down payment for our new house. We moved a mile away and kept the condo as a standalone rental property. We now rent out that condo in the middle of Hyde Park, a great neighborhood, close to the university so there's always a good selection of tenants.

Real estate absolutely is always about location, location, location. We're continuing to get $500 a month in passive income *after* all of our expenses are paid, including our mortgage, assessments, insurance, and taxes. This income is specifically allocated to our daughter's college savings fund, and thus she now gets $6,000 per year toward her college account from this activity. The investment now allows us to trade less of our precious hours for dollars through our jobs. My investment into the condo has also met my needs, and now our needs, in several different ways beyond the dollars over the years; the condo has provided us with a place to call home, flexibility in how we utilize or rent the space, and countless memories.

My experience also exemplifies the power of the SIPPin' & Livin' strategy on the investing side. Now, you might say, "Charisse, I don't have $50,000 to put down on that condo, and I definitely don't have that amount saved up." That's fine. You might not start there. But you can minimize your living expenses. I know you can do that.

You can do that by minimizing high-cost debt or by sharing housing expenses with a roommate. Should you decide to get a roommate, you must take the responsibility of vetting that the person moving in with you is financially and emotionally stable. You sure don't want to be bunking with anyone who will create drama in your life! So put in your due diligence, not only by running background and credit checks on potential roommates, but spending some time talking with them before you make a decision. Get a feel as to whether you'll get along under the same roof for a while.

Even if you don't have the money to buy a condo, that's okay. At first, I didn't either. When I lived in New York City, I experimented with having roommates because I couldn't afford to buy anything when I first got out of college. But I still wanted to limit my housing costs to 25 percent or less of my gross income. So for the first six years I lived in Brooklyn, I always lived with two roommates. New York is so incredibly expensive that most younger people there have roommates, so it's not a novel choice but still a financially astute one.

However, if you're not living in a city where the cost of housing is expensive, you should still consider minimizing your housing expense. Housing is by far one of people's top household expenses. If you can hold housing costs to less than 20 to 25 percent of your gross income, it's going to dramatically change how much you're able to put money into savings and investing and will put you in a power position when it's time to take advantage of opportunities like buying your first or second home or starting a business.

The point is to create the kind of extra dollars that you'll need and want so you can manifest some of those big dreams and have the kind of tangible wealth that you want. Remember that your situation will be unique, especially considering that certain expenses have risen exponentially since the 1980s. Education and childcare costs, for example, have risen 90 and 49 percent respectively from 1983 to 2018,[28] and can represent a big portion of your family's expense base as well. Whatever situation you find yourself in, I want to ensure that you're not hamstringed or caught off guard by a lack of resources. Yes, it takes sacrifice. Yes, it takes the vision that we talked about earlier. Remember, you must be the CEO of your wealth, and your dreams can happen for you.

The reason why the SIPPin' & Livin' strategy works well is that by its very nature it focuses you on the big decisions around the SIPPin' first. What do I mean by this? If you first focus on allocating some of your money toward these buckets, and then the Livin' categories, you'll have the opportunity to make large, tangible wealth-building strides in your bank account over time.

As opposed to figuring out how you can save $3 a day by cutting out your coffee intake, I am an advocate of focusing more on the big buckets of SIPPin' first. I am not saying that the little expenses don't add up, but it's the big decisions that are going to lead to way more money in the long run than some of these small dollar decisions every single day. Said another way, I'm a big fan of having that latte after you focus on the bigger decisions of saving, investing, paying down debt, and protecting your assets.

Go ahead and treat yourself to some of the small dollar indulgences if that's what you want to do, because you've put in the work up front. No guilt and no shame necessary as you drink up!

The SIPPin' & Livin' allocation strategy is an action-oriented strategy that can help you change how you approach your income, and ultimately build tangible wealth regardless of whether you are single or married, with kids or without.

Build Confidence

Armed with an action-packed allocation strategy, the final part of developing an investor mindset is building your confidence. One of the best ways to do this is to surround yourself with people who can help you achieve your wealth goals. We've covered assigning your financial advisor to act as the COO of your wealth back in Chapter 4. A survey from Prudential, *Financial Experience & Behaviors Among Women,* validates my suggestion. It found that "more than half the women who use an advisor (53 percent) consider themselves on track or ahead of schedule in planning and saving for retirement, versus only 23 percent of those who do not use an advisor."[29] If you feel on track or ahead of schedule on your tangible wealth goals, that helps you to keep moving toward them with less fear.

The other part of building confidence, and thereby executing on your wealth goals, is to surround yourself with people who can help you minimize your tax expenses. Enter in good tax accountants and good tax advisors. A good accountant should specialize in the laws, rules, and regulations for the preparation and calculation of your federal, state, and local taxes. A good tax advisor should develop very personalized strategies that help you minimize taxes related to your real estate and other investments. These experts could be one and the same, but consider having two separate experts, one in each field. Whomever you choose should be someone you trust. Hiring experts helps you protect your assets.

Building confidence also comes from having a solid infrastructure for your investments and savings accounts. By infrastructure, I mean the accounts and tools that hold your tangible wealth and allow you to easily make transactions when you desire. You will need a banking relationship with a local brick and mortar bank (e.g., Chase, Bank of America, or one of many smaller banks), credit union, or online bank, such as CapitalOne, plus an individual brokerage account with a firm such as Vanguard, Schwab, or Fidelity. A solid infrastructure starts and ends with technology and service, so choose companies that stay up to date with these capabilities. Automate your investments if at all possible.

A T. Rowe Price study found that when employees are auto-enrolled in retirement plans, plan participation almost doubles and successfully gets participants who might not have otherwise saved for retirement to save.[30] On the other hand, people who are auto-enrolled in retirement accounts tend to contribute less to their accounts than people who opt in and set their own savings rates and investments. Those who opt in usually have better investment results. It's better to have a retirement account than not have one at all, but it's even better to be the active CEO of your wealth.

Also, as a consumer, you will make more informed choices when you collect the right information in the moment when you are making decisions. Digital and mobile technology makes this process feasible on a mass scale. Use your mobile dashboards to your advantage.[31] Whether you are using mobile technology to track your retirement account, trade in your brokerage account or simply to consume market information, the data suggest that digital technology helps you make better decisions.

Another part of getting good infrastructure is ensuring that you leverage your banking or credit union relationship to achieve your goals. Rightfully, you might have a lack of trust for traditional financial institutions, but I want you to use them to *your* advantage. The Paycheck Protection Program (PPP) that provided forgivable small business loans to owners during COVID-19 exposed how important it was to have a good relationship with a bank if you wanted to get a loan. We now know that many PPP small business loan borrowers received loans because of their relationship with their banker.[32]

On the personal banking side, you may not realize it, but you spend a lot of money in banks by putting your deposits there. Banks are making money off of you hand over fist because they're turning around and lending out your money to other people. So, if your deposits are benefiting the bank, then make sure you demand that your bank gives you high-quality service and access to financial products that help you meet your needs.

Getting access to good financial products and money at inexpensive rates, for example, should always be top of mind for you. While you might be focused on eliminating that $12 overdraft fee, spend more time getting the best rate on your mortgage or home equity loan, to save yourself thousands of dollars over the years. Better yet, find out if your bank or credit union will provide you with an available line of credit if you want to, for instance, start a business, as opposed to drawing down your personal savings. I also have a credit union account because the service is top notch, and I feel like I'm a valued customer.

The last piece of infrastructure that should work its way into your investor mindset are exchange-trade funds (ETFs), which fall in the "stocks" asset class. ETFs were developed in the late 1990s and early 2000s but really have become popular over the last ten years. Instead of buying and selling individual stocks, or having someone do so for you, an ETF is a "basket" of assets, such as stocks, that trades the same as if you were to buy one stock, like, let's just say, Nike. By removing the human element, the fee to you as the end consumer is a lot lower. So if I have a lot of money in stocks, for instance, through a mutual fund, I might be paying 1 to 2 percent in fees on that mutual fund, whereas in an ETF, I might pay as little as 0.25 percent. And this is part of my "big decision" approach that I talked about early in the chapter wherein how you invest (e.g., ETFs over mutual funds) can save you large sums of money over the long run. I've been investing in ETFs for years, and I've saved thousands, not hundreds, of dollars on fees.

Also, unlike mutual funds, which give you less flexibility in trading at the price you want because the price resets once a day, ETF prices change continuously throughout the day, so you can trade an ETF at any moment of the trading day, just like a stock. You can purchase ETFs in your retirement account or individual brokerage account; ask your financial advisor which ones they can purchase on your behalf.

When I worked at J. P. Morgan in the early part of my career, I was the person picking stocks on behalf of large institutional clients. But that approach is expensive. Since then, technology has gotten so good that ETFs can imitate how the broad stock market is performing, so that you get market returns without paying high fees.

The bottom line is that ETFs are a powerful investment vehicle to add to your portfolio, and I recommend buying them over mutual funds 90 percent of the time. The only time to consider not purchasing ETFs is when you do not mind paying the additional fees to get access to an all-star fund manager who has significantly beaten the market return over a very long period of time.

The proliferation of ETFs has allowed robo-advising platforms such as Betterment, Ellevest, and Wealthfront, for instance, to explode over the last several years. If you are unconvinced that the fees for a human financial advisor are worth it, then you might find solace in these newer technology, robo-advising platforms, which have significantly lowered the cost of getting financial advice.

And if you want to invest in stocks without any advice, you can trade through your brokerage firm or, easily and less expensively through platforms such as Acorns, Stash, and Robinhood. If you're not familiar with platforms like these, let me break it down for you. In Acorns, which I use, you can make automatic daily, weekly and monthly investments. With its "Round-Ups" feature, every purchase you make can become an investment into a portfolio of ETFs.

Here is how a Round-Up works: if I spend $4.35 on a bottle of lotion (I like my skin moisturized), Round-Up will "round up" my purchase to $5.00, put the extra $0.65 in my account and keep track of each Round-Up until the total is greater than $5.00. After your total exceeds $5.00, Acorns automatically transfers the money to your Acorns account and invests the money into a portfolio of ETFs, which you choose when you set up the account. As such, Acorns lets you invest without thinking about it and funds these investments whenever you spend money with a debit or credit card.

Technology platforms like Acorns take the work out of investing, making it much easier to execute on an allocation strategy such as the SIPPin' & Livin' one that I shared. Whatever infrastructure works for you, make sure it makes your life easier and provides access to the products and services that grow your tangible wealth.

After you build the foundation of your infrastructure, you'll move into maintenance mode, leveraging that infrastructure to execute on your wealth goals. That's when your confidence will really blossom, and there's no looking back then—watch out, now!

Chapter Takeaways

Developing an investor mindset takes time, intention, and hard work. But if you're not going to invest in you, then who will? Remember what I mentioned as a prolific myth in Chapter 2: wealth is not acquired by hard work, but by luck or inheritance. Well, your efforts to develop the investor mindset will be living proof that busts that myth wide open. You can do so by becoming the CEO of your wealth, and assuming the personal responsibility to define your dreams and aspirations. I have shown you how to become a visionary with a vision board, take action through the SIPPin' & Livin' allocation strategy, and build confidence by surrounding yourself with an A-team and solid infrastructure. I'm telling you, developing an investor mindset is one of the ways that wealthy people get and stay wealthy. They invest in themselves and reap the returns. I ask you:

What elements of the investor mindset can you act on so that you will become the CEO of your wealth?

It can sometimes feel very overwhelming to get started, and this is natural. But you can move past this overwhelming feeling by focusing on the benefits. And the benefits of an investor mindset are plentiful. First, the mindset will help you seize opportunity, making your dreams and aspirations a reality. Second, you'll capture the freedom and personal power that comes with this investor mindset. Third, it will focus you on getting a return for your actions toward the life you want, which is exactly what investors do.

I've seen this mindset in spaces both professionally and personally, and I've shared it with hundreds of women. It worked for them and it will work for you if you work at it. Now is a good time to remind you of the first thing I asked at the beginning of the book—Imagine somebody calling you a Wealthy Girl. How would you feel?

Soak in that feeling, because developing an investor mindset will help get you there. Then, like my mom did for me, you can pass on your investor mindset to your family members, creating an intangible intergenerational wealth effect that transcends time.

Table 1.ILLUSTRATIVE SIPPIN' & LIVIN' ALLOCATIONS AT EACH INCOME LEVEL ON ANNUAL BASIS

Presented in Percentages on the top and in dollars on the bottom

ANNUAL SALARY					
Gross Income	$30,000	$55,000	$75,000	$150,000	$200,000
In Percentages					
SIPPin'					
Savings	5%	5%	7%	10%	8%
Investing	0%	10%	13%	15%	16%
Paydown	12%	10%	7%	6%	6%
Protection	8%	5%	4%	3%	3%
Total SIPPin'	*25%*	*30%*	*31%*	*34%*	*33%*
Living					
Taxes*	15%	22%	26%	30%	33%
Housing	35%	25%	23%	15%	15%
Charitable Contributions / Tithe	5%	5%	8%	10%	10%
Everything Else	20%	18%	13%	11%	9%
Total Living	*75%*	*70%*	*69%*	*66%*	*67%*
Total SIPPin' & Living	100%	100%	100%	100%	100%

	In Dollars				
SIPPin'					
Savings	$1,500	$2,750	$5,250	$15,000	$16,000
Investing	$0	$5,500	$9,750	$22,500	$32,000
Paydown	$3,600	$5,500	$5,250	$9,000	$12,000
Protection	$2,400	$2,750	$3,000	$4,500	$6,000
Total SIPPin'	*$7,500*	*$16,500*	*$23,250*	*$51,000*	*$66,000*
Living					
Taxes	$4,500	$12,100	$19,500	$45,000	$66,000
Housing	$10,500	$13,750	$16,875	$22,500	$30,000
Charitable Contributions / Tithe	$1,500	$2,750	$5,625	$15,000	$20,000
Everything Else	$6,000	$9,900	$9,750	$16,500	$18,000
Total Living	*$22,500*	*$38,500*	*$51,750*	*$99,000*	*$134,000*
Total SIPPin' & Living	$30,000	$55,000	$75,000	$150,000	$200,000

* *Reflects illustrative and approximate tax rate, unaffected by deductions. Your individual tax rate depends on filing status and taxable income. Consult www.irs.gov for more information.*

Step 4: Run Wealthy Experiments

WITH AN INVESTOR MINDSET now at the forefront, you are ready to run *wealthy* experiments. An experiment is a procedure, usually scientific, undertaken to make a discovery, test a hypothesis, or demonstrate known facts.[33] So I want to introduce the concept of a wealthy experiment. These experiments are all about making discoveries about your wealth, both tangible and intangible. Like most scientific experiments,[34] wealthy experiments also involve reaching an outcome through trial and error.

These wealthy experiments allow you to test a hypothesis about whether you can achieve some kind of wealth in a particular way. A positive outcome—tangible or intangible—should always be one of the hypotheses that you seek to test. When you run your wealthy experiments, you are effectively pursuing wealth in a way that honors the art of testing, learning, and growing.

I ran a series of wealthy experiments when I went searching for love. I had been out of a long-term relationship for seven months, and I was trying to muster up the courage to date, and eventually love, again.

I started first with a small experiment. I decided to openly ask my family and friends to keep their eyes and ears open for anyone who might be a good fit for me to date. Before this point, I was not ready to vocalize one of my heart's deepest desires with the people closest to me. I was now prepared to ask for help and allow myself to be vulnerable. Even though they knew I wasn't dating anyone, they figured that I had my dating life in control. Why should they have thought anything differently? I had no trouble asking for help in other areas of my life; if I were interested in a job, for example, I would ask my family and friends for referrals for that job without hesitation. Asking them to help me find someone special reminded me of how important it was to ask my close-knit circle to help my love life. Their positive response reassured me that I had the universe working with me. Boldly asking for what you want is a wealthy experiment because it often means overcoming fear and vulnerability to achieve your specific goals.

In addition to asking my family and friends to keep their eyes and ears open for Mr. Right, in 2010 I decided to join Match.com. Even though online dating was becoming more socially acceptable, at the same time, it still had some stigma attached to it. I'd hear people make statements like, "What's the matter, you can't find a date in the real world?" For me, however, I wanted to increase my pool of eligible bachelors efficiently while sparing me the drama of dealing with foolery at the club or other events. I figured that I could cut through the riffraff of dudes and hopefully have a lot of fun in the process.

I ultimately decided to pay $39.99 for my three-month Match.com subscription because I wanted to test the platform before spending any more money. I talked on the phone with three people before I got a wink from George Johnson. We began to establish this excellent email banter, which quickly moved to the phone. George was getting ready to start school at the University of Chicago Booth School of Business, which I had just graduated from a month before we connected on the platform.

George was from Connecticut, and since I was from New York, we vibed on being transplants in other cities. When we started planning for our first date, he confessed and told me that he wasn't quite in Chicago yet, and still living in San Francisco. He told me that he wanted to get a head start on dating before his arrival. I thought, "Wow! If this guy is this much of a planner around his love life, then that's probably a good sign for me."

When George eventually got to Chicago a month later, we began to go out on dates a few times a week. However, I was very upfront with him that I wanted to date several people at the same time and simply have fun. I wasn't in the head or heart space for anything too serious with anyone. I was as free as a bird and feeling great about being unattached.

Fast forward three months: I reached a point where I decided that I wanted to date someone else more exclusively. (I'll call this other guy Benny to protect his privacy.) So George and I stopped seeing each other. A month later, I found out that Benny had a tremendous temper, and our relationship quickly dissolved. Gulp!

As the Christmas holiday approached, I shared with my family, "You know, that George was an excellent dude. He was incredibly warm, compassionate, smart, funny, and fine." However, because I had ended it with him, I knew that it would be on me to reach back out to him. I was scared. I thought he wouldn't want to see me again because I had told him just a month ago that I didn't want to date him anymore.

But, in a true spirit of vulnerability and experimentation, I reached out to George over email and wrote, "Martin Luther King said to us the day we become silent about things is the day we die. I had a perfect time with you. I'm no longer seeing that other guy. I know that you might not want to talk to me again, but if you are open to it, I would love to meet you for tea." George replied in about an hour and said, "I'd love to meet." I pulled out MLK to go after what I wanted. It worked. We rekindled our initial spark, this time exclusively. George Ivison Johnson became my husband. We got married in September 2013.

Before I met George, I experimented with asking my family and friends outright to help with my love life. I experimented with Match.com, which turned out to be the best $39.99 investment I ever made. I experimented with dating other men while I dated George. I experimented with my innermost fear of rejection when I reached back out to George. I ran several wealthy experiments in different ways over that nine-month period, which resulted in one of the most significant contributors to my wealth: my husband George, an invaluable asset to my life.

My experimentation to obtain something wealthy came out of genuine desire and yearning. What types of wealthy experiments do you want to run to go after those desires when you think about your passions?

The following are different examples of how you can use different situations to run wealthy experiments: cases of necessity, teaching moments for children, and times when you just want to pass the wealth forward even though you don't know what the outcome will be. I will provide a few examples of what I did to run a wealthy experiment in these situations.

Necessity Breeds Wealthy Experiments

One of the most effective times to run a wealthy experiment is when you need to. The two times when I needed to do so most were when I was out of a job.

The first time I found myself out of a job was self-inflicted. I made the tough decision to close my business officially in 2014, and thus found myself without work. (I will come back to the full story about this business later.) For now, you should know that I was pretty depressed. As I talked about earlier, that's when I started seeing a career coach. My coach encouraged me to use my setback to move toward a new path. To get there, I would need to experiment with different approaches and opportunities that fit my needs. Because I worked for myself the prior four years, I did not want a regular nine-to-five job or nine-to-five hours.

Since making money was (and still is) important to me, I also needed to make some money. Saddled by my self-pressure, I needed to contribute something to our household, mostly since my prior entrepreneurial endeavor drained a chunk of our finances. I also needed something that could cater to my unique strengths in asset management and entrepreneurship, in part to help build back my confidence. I needed to dictate the job opportunity on my terms.

I concluded that independent consulting would be a plausible path forward. I started networking over coffee with people in both my Yale and Chicago Booth alumni networks and sharing my goals with family and friends. Once I told a few people about what I needed, one particular door opened: a fellow Chicago Booth alum told me about an asset management career fair happening a week after our coffee chat. I attended the career fair and met a vice president at a small asset management firm based in

Philadelphia. We had a few phone calls, and she told me that they wanted to bring on someone full-time in Philly.

Living in Chicago at the time, and one year into our marriage, I contemplated taking the full-time role. Eventually, George and I decided that moving to Philadelphia was not the right move for our life. Still, the vice president said that she wanted me to speak to their CEO.

I went into the phone conversation prepared to let the CEO know that I appreciated getting to know her colleagues. As we talked, I took a leap of faith and asked the CEO, "Would you consider bringing me on as an independent consultant?" I had no idea what she was going to say, especially since I knew that the CEO wanted a full-time hire.

To my complete shock, she said, "Yes, I'll think about it. Send me a proposal." So I Googled "sample proposals independent consultants," because I had never written a consulting proposal in my life. I downloaded an online template and wrote a proposal that allowed me to work a very flexible consulting arrangement, pricing it at a rate that met my needs. I charged a flat fee of $5,000 a month for four months. If I worked efficiently, I estimated spending 20 hours of my time on this work, resulting in an implied rate of $250 per hour. I could live with that. Because I knew the industry very well, the price reflected my intention to minimize my time and maximize my value.

When I had a follow-up call with the CEO to discuss the proposal, she immediately said, "Oh, this is a great price!" Her immediate reaction indicated to me that my price was too low! I then responded, "Oh, that's the after-tax number. Since I have to pay my taxes as an independent consultant, the pre-tax number is $7,500 a month." At that moment, I experimented with changing the price to my consulting gig to drive more tangible wealth for myself. The wealthy experiment worked because I was quick on my feet, knowing that I could extract more value for the service I offered. Lastly, I had nothing to lose. All she could say was "no." I thank God that she didn't.

When you desperately need something to work out, especially after experiencing a setback like I did, you should run wealthy experiments. The outcome may be different than what you expect it to be, and that's quite all right, because you just may get more than what you need.

When you run a wealthy experiment out of necessity, bring other people into your journey. While you should network with people when you don't need a job, when you're up front about your situation's urgency, people are usually spurred to help you in a very concrete way. And start with those closest to you.

When I told George what I needed, he immediately offered his support. My wealth pursuits became his wealth pursuits. Since George already had a steady nine-to-five job, we decided that a part-time consulting arrangement would help me gradually get my swagger back in working for someone else. When you let people help you in your time of need, you bust open one of the big myths we discussed in Chapter 2: wealth is the result of individual achievement. Remember, wealth is not created alone.

Without George taking one for Team Johnson (that's us) and then getting support from my network to explore the realm of possibilities, it would have been challenging to secure my part-time arrangement. I agree wholeheartedly with the late Ruth Bader Ginsberg, the second woman to serve on the U.S. Supreme Court, when she said, "If you have a caring life partner, you help the other person when that person needs it."[35] I hope you are vulnerable enough to ask for the help that you need in your journey as well, whether from a partner or those in your network.

Unfortunately, not all wealthy experiments work out the way you want them to.

Failed Wealthy Experiments

You might also find yourself in a situation when a wealthy experiment goes wrong. About a year into my part-time independent consulting job in Philly, I was ready to take on a full-time role in Chicago. One of my former professors from Chicago Booth shared a unique opportunity with me at the Chicago Infrastructure Trust, a standalone nonprofit founded by executive order in 2012 by former Mayor of Chicago Rahm Emanuel. The goal of the Trust, as it was known, was to provide an alternative source of funding that would be used to attract private sector funds to rebuild the city's aging infrastructure.

The Trust embodied a wealthy experiment's essence because it attempted to use nontraditional financial resources for the City's greater good—true asset creation. And, I bought into the idea! After several meetings with the CEO, I was offered a director position and subsequently joined the Trust in December 2014. I envisioned myself spending at least a few years with my Trust colleagues to work on impactful, innovative, wealth-building projects across Chicago.

Nine months into the role, I got a morning call from the Trust's CEO that I shouldn't come to work that day. Along with the CEO and most of my colleagues, I was let go due to the Trust's precarious financial outlook. I knew that the situation was suboptimal, but I was still surprised that I was let go, and at such lightning speed. I learned later that the Trust imploded as a result of other political dynamics at play.

Nonetheless, here I was, out of a job *again*, for the second time in two years. My wealthy experiment to take a chance and devote my talents to a seemingly innovative, new opportunity went bust. With some distance from that situation, however, I now realize that my failed wealthy experiment was bound to happen; The Trust was not structurally set up for long-term success.

I did get signals—unreturned emails, vague explanations on the organization's financial state, and the feeling in my gut that things were spiraling—that should have made me much more prepared for its inevitable implosion. But if I'm honest with myself, I chose to suppress those signals in hopes that things would work out for *me*. I experienced denial in its finest form.

Nonetheless, I found myself heartbroken at the time. At first, I was too embarrassed to file for unemployment. I then spoke to my Dad, and he confided in me about his own unemployment story as a young adult. He told me to keep my head up. He also reminded me that when I worked at the Trust, I paid into unemployment benefits should I ever need them. I will never forget his words: "There's no shame in being unemployed. There's only the shame that comes with not doing anything about it." I marched right down to the unemployment office and rightfully stood in that line. Over the months that followed, you should have seen the smile on my face when those unemployment checks hit my bank account.

When your wealthy experiments go bust, have your moment of embarrassment or disappointment. But don't stay there long. Even if the wealthy experiments do not work out, there will be so many learnings that you can acquire through the process of experimentation. These learnings might not be evident in the heat of a failed experiment, but they will allow you to mature and grow in unexpected ways. I had so much more empathy for the unemployed and gained a deeper understanding of the unemployment system.

I also met amazing colleagues and clients at the Trust, and several of those relationships forged into strong friendships. We all are bound by that experience, the good and the bad, in a way that no one else will ever know. Following our termination, we helped each other pursue our respective goals.

One of my friends from the Trust network introduced me to Next Street's founders immediately after the Trust implosion. I spent two months getting to know Next Street, a forty-person consulting firm headquartered in New York City searching for a director to launch their Chicago office. My Trust experience, though short, prepared me for this role like nothing else because of the breadth and depth of relationships I had built over the previous nine months.

Furthermore, I also developed an intricate under-standing of Chicago's public and private institutions, Next Street's primary client base. My failed wealthy experiment provided me with an understanding of government structures and systems and a solid foundation for my next gig.

You may not immediately understand *why* the failed wealthy experiment happens, but I assure you that clarity will come with time. Typically, the learnings from a failed experiment will help a future experience, and thus you should reflect on those learnings. Specifically, you should go back to your initial intention of pursuing the wealthy experiment, evaluate what worked and what didn't work from the experiment, and then channel your future efforts toward your new goals accordingly.

In my case, for example, I knew that I still wanted to do something innovative, entrepreneurial, and focused on building wealth. I also knew that I did not want to be at a nonprofit organization nor overly wedded to government politics and bureaucracy. Next Street appealed to me because most of its revenues derive from consulting services to broad public and private institutions to help them create vibrant cities for small businesses, especially those led by women and people of color.

For example, the Chicago Community Trust, one of the top ten community foundations in the country, hired Next Street to conduct rigorous research on the flow of capital and services available to entrepreneurs and small businesses in Chicago.[36] Our research led to the launch of several equity and debt funds to provide capital to business owners of color in Chicago.

I've now been at Next Street for five years. As a managing partner, I run the firm's day-to-day operations with two others. Next Street has provided me with a unique platform to pursue my wealth goals in a different yet more powerful way than I anticipated initially—by both managing a small business and supporting other entrepreneurs and small businesses at the systems level around the entire county.

Finally, after a failed wealthy experiment, take some time to have some fun and decompress as you need. In between getting laid off at the Trust and starting at Next Street, I spent time taking an improv class, going on long strolls along the lake, and sleeping past nine a.m.

Done well, a failed wealthy experiment forces you to reflect, pivot, and move in the direction that lines up with your wealth goals. If nothing else, failure will check your ego and provide a dose of humility. Since research shows that the best leaders are humble leaders,[37] failed wealthy experiments can refine your leadership attributes. I've seen failed wealthy experiments play out positively in my life, and I know it can do the same in yours too.

Wealthy Experiments with Kids

Your pursuit of wealthy experiments can also provide your children with an early mindset for experimentation. In doing so, you will help your children build cultural capital, which comes from being exposed to a diverse set of experiences, whether art, culture, world travel, or non-traditional learning environments. As adults, cultural capital plays out in our ability to network with people with a similar body of knowledge and experiences. Those interactions provide access to job opportunities or unique experiences. And for kids, "evidence suggests that the cultural capital passed on through families helps children do better in school. The education system values the knowledge and ways of thinking developed by acquiring cultural capital, both abstract and formal."[38] Thus, cultural capital helps your kids think differently about the world. Kids can use that foundation to excel in traditional educational systems, which breeds credentials and access to an economic opportunity down the line.

My parents sowed the seeds for my penchant for wealthy experimentation. One particular wealthy experiment that left an imprint on me in many ways involved a trial vacation to Londonderry, Vermont. When I was eight years old, my parents wanted to take us away on vacation, but their plans were thwarted. When one of my mother's colleagues, Veronica Coleman, asked her about her vacation plans, my mom mentioned that were staying home for the summer.

Veronica responded with an invitation, at no cost, to let our family use her summer home in Vermont. My dad thought Veronica was crazy because there was no way that a person would just let someone she didn't know that well borrow a family summer home in Vermont, of all places.

My dad was very hesitant, but somewhat reluctantly agreed with my mom to take Veronica up on her offer. On the day of our departure, my dad got cold feet, and for good reason. Outside of the fear that Veronica's vacation home was a total wreck, Vermont was a predominantly white-populated state, and, at the time, Londonderry, Vermont had six Black people in a tiny town of 1,516.[39] We knew no one in Vermont, and no one in my parents' inner circle had ever been there for vacation. Remember, Black people are rightfully fearful for their lives in predominantly white spaces, especially in the countryside.

But my mom said to my dad, "Well, what have you got to lose, Frank? If we don't like it, we can just get back in the car and drive back home. Vermont's only a four-and-a-half-hour drive from here." So my parents got us packed into the car with an escape plan in hand. You see, we didn't believe this was going to be someplace that we would like. But our curiosity propelled my parents to pack enough clothes for the week and remain cautiously optimistic. My mom's assurance to my father, brother, and me that we could try it out and come back to normal, if needed, gave us the freedom to experiment.

I remember being full of mixed emotions at the start of the drive, but then excitement pouring over me the closer we got to our destination. The houses were beautiful. The trees were lush and plentiful. We reached the dirt-paved street of the house right around sunset. At the end of the driveway, which spanned a football field and was lined with trees, was this big, beautiful house sitting all by itself and surrounded by nature. Our mouths dropped, and I remember screaming.

The keys were in a flowerpot. We were shocked—white people leave keys in flower pots in Vermont! (You've got to remember that my dad and mom grew up in Brooklyn and Harlem, respectively, where no one leaves keys in flower pots.)

When we opened the door, a note on the inside said, "Make yourself at home." We ended up staying there for two weeks in the summer of 1988, and that home became our summer vacation home for the next five years. Over that time, we also invited many extended family members to join because the house was just that big for my cousins, aunts, uncles, parents, brother, and me. Between the basketball games, fishing, alpine sledding, ice cream shop runs, grilling, movies, dinners, and merely sitting on the deck, we created unforgettable lifelong memories and experiences, contributing significantly to our wealthy family.

By the time I was fourteen, Veronica had told us that her kids wanted to use the summer house since they now had their own families. The implication was that our big family wealth experiment had come to an end, as Veronica offered our summer vacation weeks to her children.

The next year, however, Veronica let me know that she wanted to have quality time with her young grandchildren in her summer house. She asked me if I wanted to babysit five of her grandkids for a week. Knowing how much fun I had as a kid in that house, I immediately said that I wanted to join them. But, I also asked if I could bring my cousin Benasha with me to help babysit. Benasha is one of my cousins who used to come to Vermont with us on our family vacations, so she knew the house very well.

Veronica didn't hesitate to respond with a "yes." She said that she would pay each of us $300 for the week. Benasha and I very happily and expeditiously agreed to that rate. At that age, I would have taken $50 for that job, so you can imagine my excitement with six times that amount. We babysat Veronica's grandchildren for two consecutive summers. It was one of the first paying jobs in my life, and I got the opportunity to strengthen my bond with my cousin Benasha, who has become one of my closest friends on earth.

As a result of my parents' initial experiment to travel to Vermont with us as kids, our family reaped incredible tangible and intangible wealth gains. We saved money on our annual vacation expenditures, and Benasha and I earned money as babysitters, which grew our financial wealth. We had priceless bonding time together and new experiences such as alpine sledding and devouring pure maple syrup in Vermont, contributing to our cultural capital and overall intangible wealth.

I challenge you to openly partake in wealthy experiments in front of, and with, your children. Your transparency will leave a lasting impression on them to take chances, get out of their comfort zone, and create opportunities for others to take part in wealthy experiments with them.

I believe that it is so important to foster wealthy experimentation with the next generation. It starts with children, whether your own or others in your community. Children soak up everything, as their minds are still forming and their experiences are still shaping who they will be in the world. By pursuing wealthy experiments with them, you might have a long-lasting effect on not only them, but also their kids. In doing so, you will strengthen intergenerational bonds and activate the transfer of wealth from one generation to the next.

Paying Forward the Wealthy Experiments

As you pursue more wealthy experiments for yourself and your family, you will begin to develop a penchant for creating wealthy experiments for those beyond your immediate circle. From my own experience, I can tell you that your ability to formulate wealthy experiments for others may not be so evident at first. For example, George and I unknowingly created a wealthy experiment for a young woman out of our desire to build a mobile app to disrupt the Black female haircare market.

I mentioned in Chapter 3 that I was part of a formal peer group called Management Leadership for Tomorrow (MLT), which prepared its members for business school. In 2013, three years after graduating from business school, a fellow MLT alum asked if I could spend forty-five minutes with his sister, Naa-Shorme, who had just started a blog at age twenty-two. I was thirty-three and newly married at the time.

I happily made time to talk with Naa-Shorme about her blog pursuits. I didn't think anything more of the conversation until a few months later, when she told me about her friend Tierra, who was in between jobs. Naa-Shorme asked me to talk with her about my career journey. I obliged.

At the same time, George and I explored a few new business ideas on the side, apart from our day jobs. One of those ideas was a mobile app for Black women to quickly find quality hairstylists and rate them. Even though the

Black hair care market represented a multi-billion dollar industry, it was still tough to find stylists. We envisioned a mobile app akin to a Yelp for Black hair stylists. Other comparable mobile apps were clunky and painful to use. We wanted to solve that problem, but we did not have enough personal time to properly dedicate to the endeavor. As such, we needed someone to help us to explore the market and see if there was truly a need.

By the time we spoke to Tierra, I told her about our business idea and asked her if she would be interested in doing a feasibility study to assess whether there was a legitimate business opportunity for our idea. Tierra was a liberal arts major and had no previous experience in doing market research. However, George and I agreed to work with her because she was motivated, hard-working, and open to learning as well as coaching. Also, Tierra came through my relationship with Naa-shorme, and so we felt comfortable with our arrangement. Tierra worked with us over the course of nine months, conducting quantitative and qualitative market research, helping design a proto-type for the app, and sharing her findings in a digestible way. Our relationship with Tierra was entirely virtual, as she lived in Delaware and we lived in Chicago. The virtual environment created the perfect set-up because it gave us flexibility and created efficiency. We had ongoing dis-cussions with Tierra about her research as well as what it would cost to build the app.

Because of her findings, we ultimately decided that the idea was not worth pursuing. In addition to the arrival of several new competitors in the market, the cost to build and maintain the app was too hefty for us relative to other places we wanted to invest our money.

However, George and I were pleased with the process because we got to a definitive decision. And Tierra obtained a new experience and skill set through her research efforts. During her calls with us over the nine months, we also shared with her more about the benefits of business school through our eyes. Tierra then applied to business school for herself, and I even wrote her a letter of recommendation, with glee.

Tierra was accepted into, and attended, the Goizueta Business School at Emory University, to further her interest in real estate investing. Pulling in Tierra to help with our own business interests turned into a major wealth experiment for Tierra through which she gained confidence in herself and experienced a new way of thinking. Since we also provided Tierra introductions to real estate professionals in our network, she gained access to people who could help propel her career interests forward.

Tierra is a badass, and we saw that special sparkle in her eye before many others did. So, you can imagine how proud we were to see her as the feature MBA grad to watch in 2020 *Poets & Quants*. We didn't realize the full impact we had on Tierra until we read that full article. When asked "who most influenced your decision to pursue business in college," Tierra said:

> *Charisse and George Johnson. They are husband and wife and graduates of the MBA program at the Chicago Booth School of Business. After I graduated in 2014, they gave me an opportunity to work part-time in a mobile start-up idea of theirs. I had no prior business experience, but was put in charge of market research and creating a go-to-market strategy for the product. I admired the fact that they are a successful African American couple, with strong entrepreneurial spirits. Working with them opened up my mind to new possibilities, and I knew business school would be in my future."[40]*

I was floored and humbled by reading that article. Some might say that I shed a few tears.

We created space for Tierra to undergo a wealthy experiment. In reality, we also underwent a wealthy experiment because of the joy that emanated from seeing Tierra succeed—her joy became our joy, which breeds intangible wealth beyond what we imagined.

You have the power to create wealthy experiments beyond your immediate circle and pay forward what you have learned and experienced. You should seize it because you will be able to create wealth for others.

Chapter Takeaways

Many people do not use the term *wealthy experiments* today to describe their attempts at building wealth. But I want to encourage you to use this framing going forward, given its focus on the journey instead of the destination. Running wealthy experiments can apply just as powerfully to your love life or family life as your professional career. Whichever form you choose to run, or fail, in your wealthy experiments, they will breed both intangible and tangible wealth-creation opportunities.

There is no hard-and-fast rule about how long your experiments should take. In my own life, many of my experiments have taken anywhere from one month to three months to get started. They can run anywhere from one year to several years. It all depends on how long you want to test things out, and what *outcomes* you expect.

By running these wealthy experiments, you also have the opportunity to create cultural capital and intergenerational wealth transfer for your own children or others'. With consistency in running wealthy experiments, these activities will become second nature. And then it becomes not only about you; it becomes about the community around you. So, I ask you these important questions:

- *What kinds of wealthy experiments would you like to run for yourself or for your kids?*
- *Are you running these wealthy experiments out of necessity, or to take advantage of opportunity?*

- *What positive outcome do you expect: something intangible or tangible?*

Remember, wealthy experimentation requires intentionality. It can bring forth much good fruit, and so much good into the world. And that is wealth, right?

What joy and personal power you will have! Take it from one Wealthy Girl to another.

Step 5: Start a Business or Support the Entrepreneurs and Small Businesses around You

As a WEALTHY GIRL, this next step is game-changing. I truly believe that being wealthy has to include starting a business or supporting the entrepreneurs and small businesses around you. I'm going to share my story in starting my own business in the hope that it provides a window into my game-changing moment, and that it can be one for you in your journey.

I shared in Chapter 5 that I spent six years working on my craft of investing in the stock market. In fall 2007, however, I began to think about other ways to generate wealth. I had an epiphany one day when I was sitting at my desk. It dawned on me—no, it *hit* me so hard that I nearly fell out of my chair one day. There I was, investing in public companies here in the United States, but all of these companies at some point in their lifespan were much smaller companies. By the time they become public, a lot of the wealth created has already accrued to the founders and private shareholders, including employees and investors, who share in the company's profits and a portion of the company's overall valuation.

While my journey at J. P. Morgan over the last six years was informative and very helpful in honing my professional chops in the world of stock market investing, I began to think more broadly about wealth creation. I wanted to work with the private companies before they even became public.

At the same time, I started thinking about my career path. My manager was grooming me to become a portfolio manager, but I could not envision myself being a portfolio manager twenty or even ten years down the line. I simply did not hunger for a long portfolio management career. Even if I stayed, I knew that without a burning passion I would not be as successful as others who possessed a deep devotion to that role. I started to internalize that wealth creation existed beyond the public markets.

I then decided to go to business school to help ease my transition into the entrepreneurship world. I decided to apply to business schools with a strong reputation in entrepreneurship: the Stanford Graduate School of Business, the University of Chicago Booth School of Business, and the Wharton School at the University of Pennsylvania, and I got accepted at both Booth and Wharton. Shortly after receiving my acceptance letter to Booth, I found out that I received one of two Amy and Richard Wallman scholarships, which covered the full cost of tuition for the two years of business school.

In getting that scholarship, I said to myself, "Charisse, this is your chance. You're going to come out of business school with no or very little debt. And you ain't married, you don't have kids, and so if there's ever a time to take that kind of a leap, it's now."

Given the scholarship, it did not take me long to decide to attend Booth over Wharton.

Still, I did not feel prepared to become an entrepreneur immediately. I initially planned to attend Booth and then spend two years working for a venture capital firm. Venture capitalists make their money by investing in high-growth companies that can generate a high return for investors. In working at a venture firm, I thought I would get deep insights into what makes high-growth entrepreneurs successful.

However, I quickly got wise advice from a classmate who said, "Well, Charisse, if you want to start a business, don't take two years to learn how to invest in one. Go ahead and start one now." I took heed. While attending Booth, I took classes focused on entrepreneurship and start-up ventures. Two months into school, I got a bold business idea: create a technology solution to help people in their twenties and thirties better manage their personal finances. The market opportunity was big and I felt that my investing background would help bring this idea to reality. Ten months later, in August 2009, between my first and second years of business school, Smarteys.com launched. I founded the company with Adrissha Wimberly, a fellow Booth classmate, Howard graduate, and former Wall Streeter. Both young Black women, Adrissha and I saw eye to eye on tackling the problem that many young adults of all races and ethnicities face: how to effectively manage their money. Adrissha became Smarteys' chief operating officer (COO) and I took on the CEO post.

Adrissha led our strategy and marketing efforts while managing the build-out of the technology. My responsibilities included setting the vision, managing our finances, raising external capital, and providing the technology product's business intelligence. We were bright-eyed, scrappy, young, and brazen to venture out on our own without much prior entrepreneurial experience. We wanted to revolutionize how young people manage their money.

For the next several years, we built and refined the Smarteys platform. The Smarteys platform provided young adults with education on personal financial management. The platform used a proprietary algorithm that told users how much of their paycheck they should put into savings, debt paydown, and spending (the Smarteys algorithm was the precursor to the SIPPin' & Livin' allocation strategy that I spoke about in Chapter 6). Finally, users could sign up for different financial services and products through the platform. We derived affiliate revenue every time a user signed up for a product or service through our site.

Through the first four years, Smarteys morphed and evolved to meet the changing market and technology demands of its users. During that time, we hired two additional employees and fifteen independent contractors. Adrissha and I received $10,000 worth of family and friends' donations to put in the business when we first started. I also put $35,000 of my own savings from working at J. P. Morgan in the business. I raised another $20,000 in debt capital from my family, and another $300,000 from fourteen investors including former colleagues, former professors, and unaffiliated angel investors in the form of convertible debt, or debt that would convert to equity if we raised additional equity capital down the line from traditional venture capitalists. While the $365,000 total we raised sounds like a lot of money, it is not a significant amount of money for a technology company, especially when stretched over years. The amount we raised pales in comparison to the millions of dollars tech companies typically raise to scale, or significantly grow revenue, margins, or users. To put this in perspective, the annual salary range for a good software developer back in 2013 was $150,000 to $175,000. Adrissha and I had to be very creative in how we spent our money, effectively bootstrapping our way forward. Just nine months after raising the last of our capital, we were down to our last $20,000 of cash in our bank account.

The business was in a precarious position: Smarteys did not generate enough revenue to pay for its expenses, even when Adrissha and I decided not to take salaries. That was a big problem. While we knew that many successful high-growth tech companies do not generate revenue, we also knew that they had to at least generate troves of users, even for free, until they could figure out how to monetize those users in the future. This is the Facebook or Twitter model. Unfortunately for us, Smarteys did not have enough revenue or users, and the company ran out of cash.

We had three options—raise additional money to provide more cash runway to grow the business, sell the company, or close it. After an arduous attempt at selling went south because it did not line up with our values, we decided to officially close Smarteys in the summer of 2014. Adrissha and I were tired and ready to move on to the next chapter of our lives. Smarteys was no longer the place where we wanted to spend our time and capital.

I am fully confident that we made a prudent business decision. And I have no regrets about spending those years of my life trying to revolutionize how young people manage their money. All in all, starting a business and running it for those four years was game-changing for me. Forming and then closing Smarteys was a humbling journey for me. I'd never failed at something that I poured my heart, soul, and a bunch of capital into *at the same time*. Despite all the pedigrees, resources, pure grit and determination, we still failed to grow a profitable business. In fact, I'd never had an endeavor fail so spectacularly.

At first, I measured my success on what the business was able to generate by way of revenue and profits. But while it took some time and a lot of therapy to come to this conclusion, my real successes for sure came in my own learnings about me and my environment. I learned that my value and brand are not ascribed to a company, even one that I started! We still made a difference in the lives of a lot of people. I started something out of nothing.

I share this story with you because it brings to light that the journey of starting and running a business fundamentally changed my life. First, I learned so much about the fast and changing nature of technology and what it takes to build a technology company. We went from having a team of developers in Vietnam to hiring a software development company in the US to hiring our own in-house developers. At the same time, I learned that you must have a person with a technology background as part of your founding team. Adrissha and I learned tech product development as we were building a technology company— one of the quickest ways to burn through money and time. Building a technology product is hard work, and you must know what you are doing from day one.

I also learned that how you capitalize your business matters tremendously. One of the main reasons businesses fail is that they don't have enough capital to sustain operations or achieve a product-market fit. And from

2009 to 2017, less than 0.06 percent of the total $424.7 billion raised in venture capital funding went to Black female founders.[41] While that statistic may be hard to believe, that capital-constrained environment explains why I and many others did not receive capital for our businesses. I had to recognize how systemic racism came into play in predominantly white venture capitalist institutions, and you should too.

The complex structural and systemic issues that contribute to these statistics can feel insurmountable and unachievable. To fix these systemic issues, our country will need sweeping legislation, tax reform, and policies of financial wealth redistribution. And while 2020 saw a plethora of venture capital funds launched that target owners of color, and some progress has been made, there is still a long way to go.

Lastly, and perhaps most importantly, I learned that the freedom, autonomy, creativity, and opportunity to impact the world I experienced while running Smarteys was unparalleled to anything I had ever felt before. I learned from my investors, partners, advisors, and employees that it really takes a community to give a business a shot at being successful. On the other hand, there are no worse feelings than the heartache and roller-coaster of emotions that come with investing your money into a business that eventually closed.

At the time, I had to remind myself to fight against Myth 1 that I mentioned back in Chapter 2: "Wealth is only what's in my bank account." I know now that I am far more than the deficit ascribed by my inability to secure venture capital funding, and I have reframed how I measure myself and my success. I have a holistic view of the entrepreneurial journey, including my learnings and the intangible wealth that I have created. I am much more comfortable holding the natural tension between my individual effort and the racist system in which I exist.

Furthermore, I channeled my subsequent entrepreneurial efforts into an alternative route that did not depend on venture capital funding. As I mentioned in Chapter 7, I still wanted to do something entrepreneurial, which led to my roles at both the Chicago Infrastructure Trust and then Next Street. Still, one of the most effective ways to obtain traditional wealth is to create alternative, non-traditional avenues for obtaining it. And I wanted to do something for only myself on the side. So, I launched my personal website CharisseSays.com in 2014, which I use to give a public life to my voice, my ideas, and my advice. Since launching, CharisseSays.com has been a lifestyle business and a space where I can be completely myself and build my personal brand. On my Charisse Says blog and social media accounts, I talk, dance, and write about all things related to wealth creation and provide advice on having the life you want. I also use the Charisse Says platform to generate additional income beyond my Next Street paycheck by offering online classes, speaking for various organizations, serving as brand ambassador for companies, writing for outlets such as American Express, and publishing books like this one.

I put my own money into building the CharisseSays. com platform. As a result, I have generated revenues above my expenses and used the profits to invest in my daughter's college education and take trips with my family. The platform has allowed me to pursue my purpose—to have an impact on this world using my unique skill set— in an effective and efficient way without an unrelenting amount of effort on my part.

The Charisse Says entrepreneurial experience has allowed me to continue feeling the good of the Smarteys experience but without feeling the bad of the Smarteys experience. While founding and running a business have been instrumental to my journey, owning and running a business is not for everyone. It's important for you to figure out if it's right for you. Owning a business can dramatically change your tangible wealth trajectory while also providing you with numerous intangible wealth benefits: freedom, creativity, independence.

Further, you can own a business by investing in one without the burden of running it. And you can also support a business in a multitude of ways, as a consumer or as a champion. My entrepreneurial journey has also led me to believe that supporting a business can be just as fulfilling as starting a business.

I want you to understand the full benefits of owning a business, investing in one, and supporting one. I have done all three and all of these experiences have been game-changing for me. I want to share the benefits of these with you. I want you to have a renewed perspective on entrepreneurship so that you see how wealthy you too can become.

Define Small Business and Entrepreneurship for Yourself

Before you can start or support a business, you've got to define what small business and entrepreneurship mean for you. These terms are often used interchangeably and simultaneously, although there is a distinction between them.

A small business is a business, meaning that its goal is to generate a profit with revenues exceeding expenses. The U.S. Census defines a small business as a business with less than 500 employees. It may have a small number of employees, or only one, or even zero employees. In the United States, 99 percent of all businesses have below 500 employees, which equates to approximately 31.7 million companies in the country that are small businesses.[42]

Of the 31.7 million, approximately 25.7 million businesses, or 81 percent, are businesses without employees.[43] These 25.7 million businesses are classified as nonemployer businesses, wherein the owners are self-employed, and the majority of these self-employed businesses are sole proprietorships. I am self-employed through CharisseSays.com, for example, and my legal status is a sole proprietorship. I have no employees and every year I must fill out a 1099 tax form because of my self-employment status. There is a wide range of small businesses in the United States and, if you choose to own a business, you must determine which one suits you. The more employees you have, the more complicated the day-to-day operations of your business will be simply because of the infrastructure you need to manage it.

On the other hand, I believe that entrepreneurship is a state of mind. Entrepreneurs often want to start something out of nothing, and they exercise this desire in starting a business or start-up. Entrepreneurs often want to take advantage of a market opportunity or problem to solve, and that desire invokes them to act in order to take advantage of that opportunity or solve a problem. But entrepreneurs are not confined to starting or running a business. You can be entrepreneurial and still be an employee within a larger company. People who fit into this category, who crave innovation within a more traditional, larger company, are called *intrapreneurs*. Research shows that being intrapreneurial, given the desire to make an impact, tends to elevate both employee engagement and productivity scores.[44]

Usually someone who starts a small business is entrepreneurial, but you do not have to be a small business owner to be entrepreneurial. I draw that distinction because I don't want to limit the ways in which you want to define yourself. Whether you classify yourself as a small business owner and/or entrepreneur, I want you to feel comfortable along the spectrum. Both of these terms are broad and mean different things.

If you've been thinking about starting a business, reflect on whether you want to be a small business owner or an entrepreneur, or both, and then ask yourself why. Talk to other small business owners, entrepreneurs, and intrapreneurs in the industries that interest you. In addition to finding out about what fuels them, ask them what they do not like about their role. Imagine that you are starting a company from the ground up. What are you doing on a daily basis? What are you sacrificing each day: time with family and friends, hobbies, other opportunities? There's sometimes a lot of glory in starting up a business yourself and being called a founder, but you must understand what goes into this role.

Also, once you start, growing a business is tough. In *Where the Jobs Are: Entrepreneurship and the Soul of the American Economy*,[45] John Dearie and Courtney Geduldig interviewed more than two hundred founders about the challenges of building businesses. Their subjects cited five challenges to growing: insufficient access to capital, difficulty finding people with the right skills, immigration policies that keep talent out, onerous taxes and regulations, and economic uncertainty. These impediments go a long way toward explaining why companies struggle to scale, and you should keep these in mind on your own journey. I know this truth firsthand, and I want you to go in with your eyes wide open.

Alternatively, you can join a team of other entrepreneurs who have already launched a business. Joining an existing team doesn't make your journey less credible or make you less of an entrepreneur or small business owner. Rather, it means that you are going to partner up with others who have the shared goal of solving a problem or taking advantage of an opportunity. Most of the early pains and growing pains that come with starting from scratch are mitigated because you've joined a company that is already up and running. Typically, these companies have gotten over the initial hump of finding out what the market needs and have the resources to meet those needs with a quality product or service.

Even though I had a co-founder in the Smarteys experience, we lacked the financial resources to scale properly. With my Next Street experience, I decided that it was better to join a small business than go through the process of starting another high-growth-oriented company like I did with Smarteys.

Whether you start your own business or join a small team, I believe that partnering with others to run the business can help make the journey a bit more pleasant, and hopefully more successful. Having Adrissha's partner-ship was one of the best aspects of the Smarteys experience. While it wasn't always easy, we figured out a way to trust each other, rely on each other, and grow as a unit.

Better yet, consider joining a worker cooperative. When you are a part of a worker cooperative, you can participate in the profits, oversight, and often the management of the organization, using democratic practices. Workers, not distant investors, own the majority of the equity in the business and control the voting shares. The Democracy at Work Institute, which was created by the U.S. Federation of Worker Collaboratives to build the field of worker cooperatives, notes that worker cooperatives keep money grounded in the local economy and build community wealth. With ownership in the hands of workers, who are usually living and spending locally, these companies stay connected and accountable to their communities.[46]

When you start or join a small business, you also must determine whether you will be an owner of the business. If you are the founder, you typically own a large percentage, if not 100 percent, of the company at the onset. As more people join, especially those in the earlier stages, the more the founders must decide how much of their ownership stake they are willing to give to other people who can help the business grow. Business ownership, defined as one's equity stake in the business, is a key incentive for many people to start or join a company in its early days. While ownership should not be the primary driver, it does matter to many people. It matters to me, and you need to decide if it matters to you.

The type of small business that you join matters as well. The media and many MBA programs will salivate over the high-growth tech companies, like Facebook or TikTok, which require venture capital funding. These examples are so-called unicorns, companies worth over a billion dollars. At the start of my entrepreneurial journey, I was a bit brainwashed into thinking that I should only aspire toward high-growth companies that could create large sums of money for their owners, employees, and investors. I know better now that venture-backed companies are not the only worthy game in town.

On the other end of the spectrum are lifestyle businesses, which help give owners independence and access to the way of life they want. Successful lifestyle businesses may not have the same high-growth trajectory as tech businesses, but they serve an important role in our economy and for the people that run them. Examples of lifestyle businesses include restaurants, laundromats, or craft businesses. They typically require less capital to start and the barrier to entry may be lower.

Finally, when it comes to what starting or joining a business means to you, you must think about whether or not your small business or entrepreneurial pursuits are a side hustle or a full-time endeavor. A side-hustle business is something you do part-time to earn extra money on the side of a full-time job. If you sell crafts on Etsy, you're most likely a side hustler. Side hustling is also known as "part-time entrepreneurship." In an ideal world, side-hustle businesses should not take as many hours to run relative to working a full-time job, but sometimes your side-hustle business may morph into a full-time business if the payoff is big enough. CharisseSays.com is my side-hustle business. The rate of growth in the number of side hustlers is far greater than for all ventures and reflects the shift in our economy to a gig economy.[47]

There is no judgment on whether you have a desire to go the side hustle route, or to go the full-time endeavor route. The important thing is that you understand which bucket you fall into, because that choice will dictate how you spend your time, what you expect in return, and what benefits you expect.

Understand Why Business Ownership Is So Important

You may be thinking, "But Charisse, you haven't told me why I should even be going down this path." Well, I'm glad you asked. Beyond the benefits from my personal story that I shared with you, the economic case for starting a small business is very, very strong.

First, small business families have an estimated median net worth, or tangible wealth, that is five times higher than that of families with a head of household working for other employers.[48] So, if you want to generate tangible wealth for your family, owning a small business is a viable path. Now, these figures are quite powerful. In Chapter 6, I talked about what it means to develop an investor mindset. There's no better way to exercise your ability to develop an investor mindset than to take a bet on yourself, to take a bet on a small business endeavor that you want to generate a return from.

I don't know about you, but five times the return based on my own efforts versus the efforts I would get toward working as an employee are really good, right? You might be saying, "Well, Charisse, I already work in an industry where I get paid a lot of money." Hey, if that's the case, then that's all well and good for you! You might be a lawyer or doctor, you might be in the entertainment or sports industry, you might be in financial services. And yes, those industries generate high income.

It's very important for you to think about the trade-off, not just for income but for true wealth. And that gets to the second point, where the case for starting a business isn't just about the money. Most people who start a business value the freedom and independence that it affords them, or the intangible wealth effect—the flexibility of their own time and schedule, and the freedom to make decisions on their own terms.

In many of my conversations with older small business owners, freedom is key. Research highlights that 51 percent of new entrepreneurs in 2018 were actually between the ages of forty-five and sixty-four.[49] I think this occurs because by that time, you've garnered some experience; you've been around the block a few times, and you've definitely earned the right to think, "Gosh darn it, I don't want to work for anybody else. I want to just work for myself!"

That's the attitude that underlies that independence of freedom and thought, that entrepreneurial mindset that really allows you to take advantage of white space and create something from nothing.

For you, running a small business might also just be about having more of your own time being dictated by the things you want to work on. When you start a business, what's urgent and important for you becomes front and center because you own it; you're vested in making it be successful. Pretty simple, right? At the same time, clearly, some people must be employees and workers. Starting a small business creates opportunities for others and allows you to put employment into the hands of others. The 31.7 million small businesses in the U.S. employ almost half of the private sector U.S. workforce.[50] Many small business owners thrive on their ability to create impact for others through providing them with a J-O-B. Small businesses are engines to the U.S. economy.

Despite the fact that small businesses play an important role in the U.S. economy, start-ups have been declining since the 1970s. According to the Brookings Institution, the share of firms less than a year old fell by nearly half between 1978 and 2011—from about 15 percent to just over 8 percent in the U.S. The total rate of business formation dropped by a similar amount over this period.[51] And, to no surprise, the 2008 Great Recession prevented many businesses from starting. Applications for businesses with "a relatively high likelihood of turning into job creators," the Census Bureau notes, are "still far below [their] pre-recession levels."[52]

So, if we have all of these trends pointing to a decline in new business, why take the plunge? First, I believe that there can be lots of opportunity when market trends are going in the opposite direction. Secondly, if you're a woman, then there are other trends that are pointing in a direction that will encourage you.

Women-owned businesses, and especially those owned by women of color, are experiencing a recent surge and seem to be bucking the overall decline in national start-up trends.

The American Express *State of Women-Owned Businesses* report states that between 2014 and 2019, the number of women-owned businesses climbed 21 percent, to a total of nearly 13 million.[53] Women-owned businesses increased at a 3.9 percent annual rate between 2014 and 2019, while the number of all businesses averaged half that rate, at a 1.7 percent increase each year.

We've come a long way since the 1970s as well. In 2019, women-owned businesses represented 42 percent of all businesses, up from a paltry 4.6 percent in 1972.[54] American Express reports that women are starting new businesses due to a combination of factors: necessity from unemployment or the inability to find quality work, flexibility to handle caregiving responsibilities as well as how and when they work, and the desire to exploit market opportunities.

And women of color are owning businesses at even faster rates. As of 2019, women of color account for 50 percent, or 6.4 million, of the 13 million total of all women-owned businesses, and grew 43 percent over the same period of 2014 to 2019. Black women grew businesses the fastest at 50 percent, followed by Native Hawaiian or Pacific Islander (41 percent), Latina or Hispanic (40 percent), Asian American (37 percent) and Native American/Alaska Native (26 percent). Women of color employ 2.4 million people and generate $422.5 billion in revenue (23 percent of total women-owned businesses' revenue of $1.4 trillion).[55] So women, and particularly Black women, are owning more businesses than any other time in history. That's encouraging because that's definitely girl power and Black girl magic in their finest form, spurring not only individual wealth but generating high economic impact across the country through job creation. When you know that others like yourself are taking the leap to start and run businesses, it becomes a little bit more believable that you can have that, too. Yes, if other women can own businesses, so can you.

That's not to say that once you get started, owning a business will be easy or that there won't be differences in performance among other women. The average yearly revenue of Black women-owned businesses ($24,000) is the lowest of any group of women of color, and significantly lower than the overall average of all women-owned businesses ($142,900). The revenue disparity is partly driven by the fact that Black women are starting more side-hustle businesses than any other group. From 2014 to 2019, Black women side-hustlers grew by 99 percent, which is triple the 32 percent growth rate experienced by all businesses over those five years. As both a side-hustler and someone who previously tried to start a company full-time, it took me much less capital to start a side-hustle business. Side-hustle revenue is also typically lower than revenue from full-time businesses.

However, not all businesses owned by Black females are side hustles, and so side hustles don't fully explain the revenue gap. I want you to be aware of several other issues that have prevented Black-owned businesses, in particular, from achieving equitable outcomes. Since Black females are growing their ownership numbers the fastest among any demographic group in the country, understanding these dynamics is very important for us all. In my day job at Next Street, where I have studied small-business environments across the country over the last five years, especially for business owners of color, our research has has unearthed that Black-owned businesses experience inequitable outcomes for a myriad of reasons, including trouble accessing traditional capital markets for financing their business due to systemic racism that pervades traditional capital markets, low levels of household wealth to fund their businesses, and lack of access to social networks that would help them get customers, employees, and investors.[56]

For example, the Federal Reserve's 2020 Small Business Credit Survey for firms with employees highlights the disparities in access to bank capital.[57] The survey found that bank financing varies significantly by race and ethnicity of the owner. Non-Hispanic white owners record the highest reported bank funding (46 percent) compared to Black owners, who are half as likely to have obtained bank funds (23 percent) and reflect the lowest level of any demographic group. Black owners are also more likely to get funding from online lenders (27 percent), and they do so because they are denied funding from traditional bank lenders and they lack relationships with banks.[58] These online lenders typically provide loans at much higher interest rates than bank lenders, and thus when a business has to pay back money it owes, it must do so at an expensive rate that ultimately constrains cash and dampens profitability.

Even the national Small Business Administration's (SBA) lending program, which is purported to drive equitable outcomes, is incredibly flawed. It was designed to encourage banks to extend loans to all small businesses, especially those underserved, like those owned by Black people, more equitably. Analysis of historical SBA lending figures, however, shows that only 5 percent of SBA lending has gone to Black-owned businesses.[59] When the COVID-19 pandemic hit, the $660 billion Paycheck Protection Program (PPP) was rolled out by Congress and the CARES Act to provide forgivable loans to small businesses.[60] This same SBA encouraged the banks that they normally underwrite loans with to prioritize business owners with whom they had a preexisting banking relationship.[61] As such, guess who did not get a sizable share of these PPP loans? You got it: Black-owned businesses, along with His-panic-owned businesses, and women overall.

Black people will not be able to rely on traditional bank financing to grow their businesses until there are some major structural and systemwide overhauls, including less reliance on credit score, a key driver of bank financing decisions, especially since the research concludes that Blacks have lower credit scores, on average, than their white counterparts.[62]

And why should Blacks rely so heavily on traditionally financial institutions when there has been a historical breakdown in trust, appropriately coined the "Trust Gap," with these same institutions? The research shows that "Black Americans historical experiences with both insti-tutional and individual racism have led them to be one of the least trusting groups in America."[63]

I believe that it will take a long time for the structural overhauls to manifest themselves. But, the year 2020 pro-vided impetus for seismic shifts. The COVID-19 pandemic has shed light on, and exacerbated, the issues affecting not only Black-owned businesses, but also businesses owned by other people of color, like no other point in recent his-tory. In June 2020, for example, research showed that Blackand Asian-owned businesses experienced particu-larly severe shocks to cash balances and revenues.[64]

As such, COVID-19 has also accelerated the need for permanent solutions to these racial disparities in small business, given that the crisis must be averted for the sake of the U.S. economy. When you compound the urgency toward action brought about by COVID-19 with the main goal of the Black Lives Matter movement to stop racial injustice, I encourage you to reimagine a better future for small businesses owned by people of color.

While I know it's difficult to reimagine that better future on a daily basis, I do find comfort in the massive numbers of women of color who are starting and growing businesses. American Express calculated that if average revenue of all women-owned firms owned by persons of color matched that of white women-owned businesses, four million new jobs and $981 billion in revenue would be added to the economy, an incredible impact. [65]

While you wait for some of these systemic and policy changes to take root, you cannot get stuck nor get too discouraged. Your urgency starts now. You cannot depend on the system to save you; instead, you and I must help each other and you must help yourself. Remember the myth I shared back in Chapter 2: wealth is only what's in your bank account. Since I want you to define yourself beyond the dollars and cents that sit in your bank account, I believe that you must subvert the system in which you exist and leverage your intangible assets in order to be successful.

For example, you can subvert traditional financing systems by seeking capital from alternative sources apart from banks and traditional financing institutions. Sources of alternative capital are crowdfunding platforms such as Kickstarter or Indiegogo, community development financial institutions (CDFIs), credit unions, and funds that offer capital in return for a share of future revenues instead of taking an equity stake in the business.

Crowdfunding campaigns "enable entrepreneurs to raise capital from individual small investors or lenders— the "crowd"—largely over the internet and on social media platforms. Crowdfunding platforms create a venue for entrepreneurs who seek capital to connect directly with potential, often smaller-scale investors, facilitating the flow of an alternative source of entrepreneurial capital that otherwise would be very costly or unmatched."[66]

I had no idea what a CDFI was until after I walked away from the Smarteys experience. The benefits of CDFIs are well-known among economic development profession-als, but less so to tech entrepreneurs. In short, CDFIs are mission-oriented organizations that focus heavily on underserved communities and provide business loans to owners who may be denied by traditional banks.

Companies that offer small businesses investment cap-ital in return for a share of the business's future revenues (as opposed to taking an equity, or ownership, stake in the business) are known as revenue-based funders. Even though Founders First Capital Partners is one of the most preeminent revenue-based firms in the U.S., you probably have never heard of it. Founders First was founded by Kim Folsom, who also serves as the company's CEO. She is a force of nature in the entrepreneurship and venture world.

Kim is also a Black female who has raised more than $30 million in institutional venture financing, created over 500 premium wage jobs, and has founded or served as a key executive for six successful ventures, including show-Uhow (acquired by Sellpoints), DriveCam (now Lytx), and Seminarsource. And her revenue-based investment fund has helped secure financing for women, and women of color.

Women have to help other women. I have been the direct beneficiary of women helping me along my Charisse Says journey as well. During my second year of running the platform, my friend and fellow Chicago Booth classmate Kia Coleman lent her creative writing and production skills to produce a ten-week online webisode series on managing money. We secured funding for the series from SoFi, a leader in student loan refinancing, who was named the exclusive sponsor.

Kia worked tirelessly to secure the production crew, manage the filming and editing process, and help launch the final product. The experience of working with Kia gave me the opportunity not only to produce a great series for the masses, but also to strengthen our friendship—a true intangible wealth gain!

If you do not have women in your immediate friend circle who can contribute in a meaningful way to your business at the time you need it, do not fret. There are women-focused small-business centers, such as the Wisconsin Women's Business Initiative or the Women's

Business Development Center headquartered in Chicago, that are funded by the SBA expressly to foster the growth of women-owned businesses. These centers provide dedicated education, training, coaching, and access to alternative financing solutions for women-owned businesses. I wish I had known about these centers when I started Smarteys as I believe that they would have accelerated my growth.

Above all, I encourage you to take a leap of faith when you take the small business or entrepreneurial journey. Whatever form it takes, expect the journey to be challenging. My faith propelled me forward like nothing else in my own entrepreneurial journey, and through all the ups and downs, I believed that I was going to see the benefits of my efforts. I could take the entrepreneurial plunge because of my faith. I could attract the right mix of investors and partners because of my faith. I could make good business decisions because of my faith. I could wind down my business because of my faith. I'll talk more about what it takes to build a faith muscle in Chapter 9.

If you're someone who concludes "It's just too hard and I don't want any part of starting or growing a business," I can understand and I will not judge you. It's draining and the journey is not for everyone. Trust me, we need your support in other ways too. You're not off the hook; there's still a role for you in the small business and entrepreneurship community, and that's to support others who are doing it.

The reason why this is so important is simple: When you support others in obtaining wealth through small business and entrepreneurship, their gains don't just accrue to their household, but in the communities that you live in. Their wealth grows your wealth, tangible and intangible. I want that for you. I want that for all of us, too.

Support Small Businesses

You are a small business customer. I know that you do not wake up every day identifying yourself in that manner. But it is never too late to start. You have the opportunity to move the economy forward by buying goods and services from small businesses.

I have already laid out the business case for why supporting small businesses matters to our economy. Now I want you to personalize your role in passing the wealth forward as a customer. Where you spend your dollars matters. One of the big myths that we talked about in Chapter 2 is that wealth is an individual endeavor. When you support small businesses in the communities around you, you contribute to collective wealth. So before you go out and purchase goods and services from large corporations, consider whether there is a small business that might offer the same product or service.

I know, sometimes the ease and convenience offered through large corporations make it so easy to buy from big box retailers, but I encourage you to buy from small businesses when the opportunity presents itself. Or, if you must, purchase the goods made by small businesses that sit on the shelves or online platforms of big box retailers (e.g., Target or Amazon). Trust me, it takes a lot of effort and a foregoing of some profits for small businesses to distribute their goods through the big guys.

I know the counterargument you might be mulling over in your mind: small businesses' products and goods usually cost more. You're right, in that sometimes they do. But price should not always be a deterrent. You typically buy things that you value, and where those things are sold matters in the equation of that value.

Remember the SIPPin' & Livin' allocation strategy in Chapter 6? If you allocate your income to savings, investments, paydown, and protection first, you can spend on the other things that you desire without regret. Furthermore, you should take a lesson from my generation, the millennials: spend money on quality products and causes that matter. "Despite the fact that millennials are coming of age in one of the most difficult economic climates in the past 100 years, they continue to be most willing to pay extra for sustainable offerings."[67] You can apply a millennial perspective to buy from small businesses, who sustain nearly 50 percent of the private sector jobs in this country.

In addition to supporting small businesses as a customer, you can support small business owners through your relationships. How many times have you gone into a restaurant and talked to the owner about their food or shared how much you liked the service? Well, I have done it on numerous occasions, and in the midst of the conversations, I've also shared ideas about where these businesses might also get more business. For example, for restaurants that I really enjoy, I'll provide the owner with recommendations on different corporate clients they might provide catering services to. In its most basic form, you have a relationship with a variety of rating apps like Yelp, and you can offer a positive rating on the food. The power of your relationships extends beyond you solely helping to get small businesses more customers or ratings. For instance, you might have a friend or family member who's starting or running a small business. If they are like me, at some point they will ask you to promote their business in some way, whether through sharing a link to their business on social media or email.

When you get these requests, please fulfill them and do more than what's asked of you.

How much more powerful would it be to amplify your friend or family member's business beyond the initial outreach you may do at launch or special occasions. I urge you to constantly keep those small business owners in your network at the forefront of your mind. Ask your friend or family member: "What are the three things you need over the next twelve months? Or can I make a connection for you in your business?" Ask the owner how you might help. Starting and running a business is tough, and your overture may be received with open arms. You should not underestimate your contribution to help move them forward.

The final way I urge you to support a business is as an investor. I talked earlier about how small businesses can use crowdsourcing to raise money for their businesses. Well, you can use crowdsourcing platforms to invest in businesses. The 2012 Jumpstart Our Business Startups (JOBS) Act made way for nonaccredited investors to make equity investments into businesses for which you receive an ownership stake. Thank you, President Obama.

Other crowdfunding platforms let you make debt investments, meaning loans that are expected to be repaid, while others (like Kickstarter, GoFundMe, Indiegogo) rely on payments for which you receive "rewards," often in the form of the product the company is preparing to produce. For instance, the lesser-known platform, SMBX, has a very attractive value proposition: "a marketplace connecting everyday investors like you with small businesses to invest in. Earn up to 9 percent interest by investing in local small businesses you love."[68] The goal of platforms like SMBX is to create a marketplace that unlocks wealth for small business owners *and* the communities that invest in them.

I know the power of investing in small businesses. I serve as a general partner in the Bulldog Investment Group (BIG), a venture fund started by Yale alums looking to invest in other Yale alums.

In December 2015, I was connected to Jay Readey, a fellow Yale alum who was working on this new fund. Jay said to me, "I'd like you to be a general partner in this new venture capital fund. The minimum investment will be $200,000 in order to be a general partner." I told him flat out, "Jay, I'm not sure who else is contributing to this fund, but I am starting a new job and I don't have $200,000 to invest."

By this time, I had been married to George for two years. In a supportive tone, George said to me, "Well, you've been talking about trying to invest in businesses for a while. Maybe this is a way to diversify our assets. We can take some of the money that we had been saving toward buying a house and put it into this venture, and perhaps put off buying a house for a little later when we can build back up; there's no rush on moving right now." Now, George and I knew that we could not invest $200,000—but perhaps we could invest $50,000. I told Jay what I wanted to invest in the fund on my own terms and at a much more reasonable level for my personal situation and my age. And I also told him that very, very few Black people have that kind of money sitting around, given the structurally racist ways in which institutions have prevented Black families (even those who went to Yale) from amassing wealth. Jay talked it over with the BIG board, and they approved my proposal. They were very intentional about getting diversity into the general partner ranks: they saw a young, smart Yalie who was also a Black female, and I saw the opportunity to access a group of older, smart Yalies who were white. We fit as Yalies. We fit on values. Ultimately, we also fit on making money and providing advice and support to Yale entrepreneurs;

we saw eye to eye on the ability to create intangible and tangible wealth.

It's important to also note that I did not have to invest the $50,000 upfront, but rather only when the Fund called my capital to make investments. I invested an average of $10,000 per year from 2016 to 2020 to fulfill my level of investment. This is a secret of venture capitalists: investors only provide the money upon a capital call, which preserves the cash in the bank account of the investor until needed.

I became one of the youngest people in this venture fund, and I served on the investment committee, which has the decision authority to evaluate and make recommendations of early-stage companies that the fund should invest in, and therefore holds significant power in the BIG fund. This experience allowed me to get an intimate view and get investment dollars into small businesses that I had a part in selecting.

My investment in BIG reflected my first foray into venture capital investing. From 2015 to 2019, the fund made initial investments of $100,000 into twenty-one companies, plus follow-on investments in a select number of these companies. BIG has several years to go before it will see returns on its portfolio, which is typical for an early-stage investment fund.

I share my venture capitalist story with you so that you clearly know that wealth isn't reserved only for white people. And, sometimes you have to force yourself into a traditional system in a different way, thereby subverting the system. In fact, you can sometimes create a new system by your presence and your power.

Find your place along the small business investing continuum. Whether you make an investment (equity or debt) in a family member or friend, invest in small business owners through a crowdfunding platform, or invest in high-growth companies as a venture capitalist, you must find a match for yourself. All of these investment paths are viable and have the potential to redefine your own wealth creation story.

I have talked a lot about both the tangible and intangible aspects of wealth. This perspective applies to supporting a business as well. You can certainly reap the tangible benefits of investing in a business through your financial return, and you should surely aspire toward that goal.

But there are real intangible benefits for supporting businesses in this manner as well: learning and joy. You will learn a lot simply by following or supporting someone else's small business or entrepreneurial journey. You will also get joy in seeing them succeed. And I want you to have that joy. I want you to know that your impact matters. I bet you're craving to have an impact these days, especially in the COVID-19 era. Well, starting a business is one of the hardest things anyone can do in their life. It is an emotionally taxing upside down, "get me off, put me back on the roller-coaster" kinda ride. When you support someone else on that journey, you are advancing their joy. But I can also personally assure you that you will get your own fill of joy just from being a part of their journey. Another intangible asset that will develop from supporting a small business as a consumer or investor is your very own entrepreneurial mindset. You will start to think about your everyday occurrences as problems to solve or as opportunities to take advantage of. It is a liberating feeling, and it only comes with starting your own journey or being part of someone else's. You begin to think differently about the world. What would it take for there to be more entrepreneurial-minded folks? How many problems could we solve collectively? How could we make sure that there is access to many of the things that we all care about?

And the best yet? You will take all of these entrepreneurial and small business experiences and pass them on to the next generation, who then believes that they can change the world. Ah, what personal power! What a wealthy life!

Chapter Takeaways

Starting or supporting a business will be game changing for your life. First, you must define, or redefine, what small business and entrepreneurship mean to you. Women own more businesses now than at any other time in history. Small businesses owned by women of color are growing at the fastest clip of any demographic group. It is an exciting time to jump into the mix. Before you plunge in with both feet, figure out what type of business you want to start and why. The case for business ownership is powerful: small businesses create jobs, spur innovation, and create tangible and intangible wealth.

> *If you have a desire to start a small business or entrepreneurial endeavor, what will help you move from idea to action? If not, what are* three things *you can do to support the small businesses and entrepreneurs around you?*

Remember, you don't have to start a business yourself to reap the benefits of small businesses. Consider supporting small businesses as a consumer, being a marketing champion through your social media posts, and investing. By supporting small businesses, you have the power to create both intangible and tangible wealth not only for yourself, but also for the communities you live in.

What's holding you back, or what will it take to propel you forward to new heights?

Maybe you could use a little bit of faith.

9

Step 6: Build a Faith Muscle

IN THE PREVIOUS CHAPTER, I shared with you how my faith sustained me during my entrepreneurial journey. Your faith can be one of your most precious assets, with the potential to generate incredible wealth over and over again in your life. As such, let me share with you how vital that muscle has been in my entire life and how you can build a faith muscle.

As you probably figured out from reading the earlier chapters, I played many sports growing up. I especially loved track and field because I was better at the sport than everything else I played, including basketball, volleyball, and tennis. I'll share more later on how I came to love track and field. For now, you need to know that I was not fast enough to get a college scholarship, but I held my own as far as high school competition was concerned. I won a few Nassau County titles on my relay team and came in third in the triple jump in the county. I tell you, excelling at something matters, even on a small scale. I know that you have places in your life like this, too. I started running on the track at age five, but it was only during my high school track experience that I learned how to weight train. In our weekly workouts, we weight trained three of our five weekly practice days. I worked hard during those weight training sessions, and during my four years in high school I developed strong, defined arm and leg muscles. I stopped running track when I graduated from high school, but my muscles have never really left me, and my arms and legs have held their tone, because of that rigorous high school training.

To this day, I love showing my arms because they're sculpted. Now, my arms have looked less toned at specific points over the last twenty years (and some might give me a side-eye and say "quite flabby"). However, with a little working out, my muscle memory kicks in, and the definition in my arms and legs snaps back pretty quickly. Trust me: I am incredibly grateful for the snapback.

Building a *faith muscle* operates the same way. According to Book of Hebrews, "Faith is confidence in what we hope for and assurance about what we do not see." A lot of people throw around the "faith" term without a proper understanding of what it means. We'll get there. For now, know that it will take you a lot of hard work in the beginning to develop the faith muscle. This is your baseline. Once you establish a foundation, your faith muscle memory will kick in when you need it, especially during challenging and uncertain times.

My faith muscle has kicked in at critical moments in my life, but there's one particular experience that stands out: when I yearned to have a baby, and it just wasn't happening. Babies represent wealth in the most tangible and intangible ways. Sure, they will hopefully become hard-working individuals who generate or inherit substantial wealth. Yet no price tag will ever be high enough to encapsulate their full value given the joy they bring to the world—babies are priceless assets.

Let's go back to 2015, two years after I got married. That's when I started praying for a child. We hadn't started trying to conceive, but these prayers emanated from my strong desire to be a mother. I try to start praying for things before I go about any action steps because I want God to be all up in the mix and ensure I'm on His path too. If God didn't see fit for me to be a parent, I wanted some time to work through this. This has always been a scary proposition: coming head-on with doing something that I want to do, and God doesn't want me to do.

Now, I'm not one of those people who hear directly from God through his voice or any burning bushes. My Grandma Shine is the only one in my life who seems to have this type of connection. She has told me countless stories of literally hearing God's voice talk to her. That's not been my experience. But, I do hear from God through other people who are close to me, sermons, prayers, music, and in my quiet meditative time reading the Bible. Every-one hears from God in their special way—trust in the unique way in which you will hear from God!

Well, I did not receive any messages that parenting was not in the cards for me—quite the opposite. In October 2015, I received two cards in the U.S. mail. One was from my former business partner and friend, Adrissha, who told me, "I know not all the prayers of your heart, but I pray them with you. As you continue to grow in marriage and career, hold tight to that 'blessed is she who believed.'" The other card came from Mama Conrad, the mother of Bethany who I talked about in Chapter 3, who shared with me, "Sometimes it is nice to see something besides bills in our mailbox. I was thinking of you and wanted you to know Joshua 1:19 states, 'Be strong and courageous. Do not be terrified; do not be discouraged, for the Lord Your God will be with you wherever you go! Blessings to George also.'"

I taped both of these cards in my journal. Had they known I had been praying and wanting a child at that moment and was struggling to convince my husband that we had to start trying now before I got too old? No. But something inside them compelled them to send me these notes because God knew I was beginning to feel down about the possibility of having a child.

The year 2016 offered little progress by way of family planning. George wasn't ready yet because he had just switched jobs, and although he wasn't traveling all the time like he used to, he wanted some time to transition into this new career and make good on his MBA investment. And it takes a minute to reconnect emotionally, mentally, and, ultimately, physically. Trust me, we needed some time to find ourselves again after several years of him traveling five out of seven days a week, which followed four years of finishing his MBA while I was winding down my business and trying to find myself again too. I now call the first three years of our marriage "Part 1: Barely Surviving."

By the time 2017 arrived, we were both ready to start trying. For a whole year, we did. While we certainly had fun with the process at times, it created a whole new level of anxiety and stress. I found myself lying on my back during sex, saying, "This might be it," and being flat-out disappointed when my period came the next month. When you repeat this emotional yo-yo, it can be quite exhausting and emotional.

To top it off, by the end of that year, my ob-gyn told us that we had "unexplained infertility." Apart from the evident sadness that came with the reality of not being able to conceive, I was heartbroken on multiple levels, from not pinpointing a cause to not controlling the outcome. I often cried as I also sat with the guilt of waiting so long. By the beginning of 2018, we started intrauterine insemination (IUI). If you're not familiar with it, it's a fertility approach that typically precedes IVF or in-vitro fertilization. IUI is a relatively low-tech outpatient procedure in which your partner's washed sperm is placed in your uterus while you are ovulating. A nurse then takes a thin, pen tip–sized catheter and shoves that washed sperm up in your uterus. Sounds romantic, right?

George and I (mostly me, given that it was my body with the eggs) underwent this procedure each month from January to August. I went to the clinic three to four times over the course of a month. Basically, I took Clomid medication to help stimulate my hormones and egg production, went for blood and urine tests, injected myself with Ovidrel to boost ovulation, and then had that catheter shoved up my vagina when my eggs were ready.

For six months, I got very good at timing my travel schedule around my IUI cycle and making all the necessary adjustments to dart over to Northwestern Fertility clinic by eight a.m. on the days when it fell on a weekday, and then dart over to work for client meetings or take calls at the hospital if the appointments ran over. Now, if you know anything about Chicago geography, getting from Hyde Park to Streeterville in the middle of rush hour, or through the snow in March and April, comes with its own set of challenges. It's at least a forty-five-minute commute on public transportation, which I took to the hospital nine out of ten times. And, George and I treated ourselves to tasty brunches when the procedures fell on the weekends. These brunches were emotionally comforting as we extended extra tenderness toward, and faith in, each other. As a result of our unique situation, we grew even closer.

I know what you're thinking, and I agree wholeheartedly: I had the privilege of schedule flexibility given my white-collar professional status and the position of authority I sat in at Next Street. I also had the privilege of Next Street's health insurance, which covered the majority of the cost of these fertility procedures, doctor bills, and medications. Schedule flexibility and health insurance reflect two necessary assets—the first intangible and the second tangible—that cannot be appreciated enough for the wealth they created in my life during this time.

I would walk into the clinic every month, hoping and praying that God would bless us. On top of the years of yearning and trying, the first six times I had to deal with disappointment, disbelief, and a challenge to my faith. When you want something really bad, you'll also go the distance. I did. Acupuncture. Check. Extra doses of folic acid. Check. Crying. Check. Limiting stress and exercising a lot. Almost check. Crying. Check again.

On the seventh IUI attempt in August 2018, I became pregnant, and Gabrielle Grace Johnson entered the world 40 weeks later on April 26, 2019. I believe wholeheartedly that I exercised my faith muscle from 2015 through 2019 up until her birth. And now that she's here, I need that faith muscle every day.

What will it take for you to build your faith muscle? Let me tell you.

Define Faith on Your Own Terms

I said I would come back to what faith means. Faith means that you are vested in the hope of a higher power beyond yourself. In my case, this power is God. My perspective is rooted in Christian theology, my lived experience, and as a personal witness to how my family and friends have lived in faith. I bring you back to Hebrews 11:1, "Faith is confidence in what we hope for and assurance about what we do not see." Faith is a belief that God, or a higher power, will provide the desires of your heart even though you do not see any evidence of those future desires today. For me, faith and God go hand-in-hand; they are inextricably linked. I cannot build a faith muscle without God's help, and my link to God is Jesus, who binds Christianity together. Said another way, "Without Jesus, I cannot get the full power of God, and thus the gift of faith, in my life." While you may disagree with my belief that God and faith go handin-hand, you probably latch on to the principle of faith, which in secular terms is hope. We can all be hopeful.

Faith also takes action. We learn in the New Testament in James 2:17, "Thus also faith by itself, if it does not have works, is dead." I've always reread this passage and connected it back to the first definition because the verse challenges me to take responsibility for the desires that I have. I take "works" to mean that you must actually live out your faith—it's not enough to cast a hope and a prayer without doing your part.

In my case, I could have let George's timeline for having a child completely dictate my desires instead of speaking up for what I wanted. Men just don't have the same biological pressure to have kids that women do, and thus George could not immediately empathize with my urgency.

I also could have continued to try to conceive the natural way in the face of our unexplained infertility. However, I took to heart the words of a mentor, age fifty, who told me that in three years, when I turned forty, she didn't want me to have any regrets about not taking action on my own reproductive journey. Another big part of building the faith muscle means accepting that *how* God provides what you want, and *when* he provides, may indeed be different than your original expectations. So I chose to take action both through prayer in faith that the outcome that I wanted would come true and through fertility options that could assist me in getting pregnant.

The last thing I will say is that building a faith muscle takes time to develop, just like getting in shape and building your physical muscles. Like anything that takes time to develop, building faith takes discipline through various seasons in your life. Faith muscles are needed most when things are not going as you expect; when things are going well, you might not take the opportunity to build the muscle because you don't seem to need it as much. According to C. S. Lewis, one of the most renowned atheists-turned-Christian, we "must train the habit of Faith." I believe that this training will continue to happen throughout your life, so there's always more to learn.

However you define faith, it can be a powerful force in your life because it will give you the assurance you need to keep going and to overcome the fear that tends to stop us from having the desires of our heart.

Faith Defies Statistics: Do What Feels True to You

If you listen to many other people and do what *they* think is best for you, it will be harder for you to exercise *your* faith muscle. Our fertility doctor told us that we should just stop trying the IUI treatments because our chances were slim; he said in so many words, "since you already tried six times, your chance of conceiving is nil." We were reminded of what the doctor told us at the beginning: the probability of success is 20 percent for each IUI cycle. Since we had just passed our sixth attempt, things looked grim statistically. He advised us to go straight to IVF since IUI had been unsuccessful.

However, we decided to go for a seventh try at IUI, against his counsel, and we also went through a half-day boot camp for IVF treatment to prepare ourselves in case the IUI didn't work out. I even scheduled the medicine to be delivered for the next month so that we could prepare adequately. We hoped that IUI would work out, but we prepared for the reality that it might not. Building a faith muscle takes hope in an uncertain future *and* action toward that future. We didn't tell anyone in our circle about this last round. We held it to ourselves. (Now, your actions may look different than mine, but whatever form, it's the act that accompanies the faith that matters.)

Throughout the entire time, family and close friends were praying for us when we did not have the strength to pray for ourselves. For instance, I specifically remember when my faithful friends Michelle and Kia prayed over me at a coffee shop. I told them how disappointed and disheartened I was due to our unsuccessful conception attempts. As my tears flowed, so did theirs, and their prayers of encouragement bolstered me.

Even the technicians who saw me during the hospital visits would constantly offer up words of encouragement like, "You will have this baby." And one of those technicians prayed especially hard for me too. She had also undergone fertility treatment and provided such comfort when I would lay there in the darkness wholly vulnerable and naked, legs spread wide open, as she took pictures of my eggs.

Statistics will sometimes paint a grim picture of the current reality based on past results. Statistics are good at describing the past but not good at predicting the future for your individual situation. Make sure you evaluate your decisions through the lens of what you think is best for you and your family, based on that faith muscle that you've developed.

Let Go of Your Timing and Expectations around the Outcome

When you want something bad enough, you want to take control of the outcome, especially if you're a control freak like me. You think that if you put in effort and time to achieve something, things should work out when you expect them to. I think that's a reasonable expectation. But life doesn't work that way. The outcome you're looking for may not come when or how you expect it to.

When George and I went for our seventh IUI treatment, it was the same day that I had to meet the painters at our new home at eight a.m. and make my nine a.m. IUI appointment. For context, this was the only appointment that George and I did not go to together; he planned to get to the hospital by 8:30 a.m. and provide his sperm. This was the only time he procured the sperm at home and transported it in a special bag to the hospital.

We were not set to move into the house until the weekend, and thus I had to drive to the house from our condo at 7:30 a.m. I begged the painters not to be late. They were still late, arriving at 8:30 a.m. I needed to have left the house by 8:30 a.m., but given their tardiness, I left the house at 8:45 a.m., racing up Lake Shore Drive and honking ferociously at my fellow drivers stuck in traffic. At 8:50 a.m., I got a call from the hospital telling me that all of George's sperm was dead. I was so distraught I almost crashed upon hearing the news. They asked me if I could have him come back to the hospital because they couldn't reach him.

I called George as he was stepping out of his Uber into an important meeting. I told him what had happened, and he jumped back into the Uber, headed back to the hospital to try again. To this day, I'm not sure what he told his colleagues, but whatever it was, I am grateful. We each arrived at Northwestern at 9:30 a.m. He procured another sample and then had to go back to work. This was the first time I would do the IUI procedure without him there by my side, holding my hand. As I lay there, all I could think about was whether I'd be done by ten a.m. for the meeting I was leading.

The fear started to creep into my thoughts, and I heard the voices saying, "With all the stress of today, there's no way this could work. You better get ready for IVF." Nothing about the morning was how we normally went about the procedure. The nurse took the catheter out of my uterus at 9:55 a.m. and, as usual, told me to be still for at least ten to fifteen minutes.

I turned off the lights and took that seemingly important call, which I can't remember anything about, on that patient table with my pelvis perched up on a little pillow to help make the magic happen. I stayed there for 30 minutes through the end of the call, and then another 30 minutes with my eyes closed, in darkness.

Fifteen days later, I was waiting for my period to come. As the days turned into a week after my usual period timing, I felt light, and I started to think about the possibility of being pregnant. I waited eight days post my usual start of my menstrual cycle, and then I couldn't wait anymore. I opened the pregnancy test in my bathroom, peed on the stick, and got the double line. Positive. Shaking, I immediately screamed, "Thank you, God. Thank you, God!"

I thought George was still in the house, but he had left. I ran out the back door in my leopard pajamas to try and catch him before he pulled his car out of the garage and drove away. Eventually he saw me in his rearview mirror. When he backed up, I told him, "We're expecting." He replied, "Expecting what?" I said, "A baby."

Sometimes even the most faithful among you will try to put time parameters on when the outcome you're seeking should transpire. In the month leading up to that last IUI appointment, my Grandma Shine, the greatest faith warrior I know, said to me, "Now, don't wait too long, Charisse." Having just turned ninety years old, she got into the habit of saying whatever she felt was necessary for the moment. I had to remind her, however, "Grandma, it's not up to me. I'm doing what I can, and it's in God's hands now." She said, "That's right, baby. I'll pray again."

Trust God's timing, and no one else's. Otherwise, the disappointment in not seeing the outcome you desire can overwhelm you.

Your Support of Others Will Build Your Faith Muscle

Faith is both individual and collective. You can do your work to exercise your faith, but your community of trusted support helps you perfect your faith because they are there to encourage you. Throughout my life, my community of support has come from my church family, including Urban Village Church in Chicago, which I have attended since 2014, and the people in my life who are faithful.

Doesn't it seem that when you want to do something so badly, there are several people not only doing it but excelling? In my case, everyone seemed to be popping out babies left and right at the very moment that I wanted one. Seeing pregnant women everywhere can cause sadness on the inside. However, I have learned that you can be sad and supportive of others at the same time. I gave my sadness over to God to hold, and He did.

God helped me to be genuinely happy for the women in my life who were pregnant. Instead of being envious or jealous, their pregnancy journey helped to encourage me because the women would say things like, "Charisse, your turn is coming," or, "I can't wait for your baby to come." I explicitly remember my dear friend Phoebe sending me a text on Mother's Day in the spring of 2018 before we even conceived that said, "Charisse, you're on your way to being a mother soon, too." Go ahead and pinch yourself too—I can't make this stuff up.

It's important to know that these words of encouragement came from my close circle of women who knew my fertility struggles. These sentiments helped me be supportive and encouraging to them as they journeyed on their own motherhood paths.

For example, I enjoyed planning one of my dear friend's baby showers because I genuinely was happy for her. Even in her own fertility journey, her faith encouraged me. Since the parents-to-be were traveling back to Memphis from the baby shower, they left us with a few of their gifts to return locally in Chicago. The only gift that we could not return was the blue baby tub. I thought about giving that tub away and even throwing it out at times in despair for my situation, but a little voice kept telling me, "One day, you will use that tub." And when my dear friend Michelle would visit, she too would say, "I can't wait for you to use that tub." Little did she know how her words helped me get through the insecurities in my mind that sometimes fed in and said, "Why are you keeping this tub, Charisse?"

Building your faith muscle often comes with spasms of unfaithfulness because you're human. And that's okay as long as the spasms are temporary. Michelle would be one of the first people to meet Gabrielle and help me wash her in that blue tub.

Now, I could not work on building my faith muscle by myself. God helped every step of the way, and He made space for support and joy for others even when I was sometimes sad by my circumstance. He was using these opportunities to build the faith muscle in me, and in the process, remove the anxiety that often comes from feeling like you will not get that thing that you want so badly.

The Outcome Serves as a Constant Reminder of Your Faith

Whether it is how you envisioned it or something different, the outcome of your circumstance will remind you of your faith. Gabrielle is the manifestation of our faith and a testament to the faith muscle I have built.

About five months into the pregnancy, we found out that Gabrielle had an extra blood vessel that pumps blood into her heart. In medical terms, she had a left superior vena cava, which usually disappears during pregnancy. The doctor told us that the extra vessel could cause heart problems and that we would have to monitor it after Gabrielle's arrival. We carried the mystery of the unknown outcome for the heart condition and the accompanying anxiety throughout the pregnancy. Oh, and I also had placenta previa, wherein the placenta blocks the cervix opening and can cause delivery complications, right up until thirty-nine weeks of pregnancy before the placenta miraculously moved out of the way.

When Gabrielle's electrocardiogram results showed "no issue" forty-eight hours after she arrived, I knew God was with us the entire way, and Gabrielle is a testament to God's faithfulness. We named her Gabrielle because it means "Strength of God," along with the middle name of "Grace" after her paternal grandmother, as well as the fact that she is filled with God's grace as well.

I sneak into my daughter's bedroom often to simply stare at her. I find myself pinching myself or tearing up a bit because I'm so grateful that she is here and healthy.

So, when it was time to celebrate Gabrielle and welcome her into the family of faith through baptism, I was overjoyed. My pastor and friend, Rev. Emily McGinley, who knew about our fertility challenges, asked George, me, and Gabrielle's godparents, Bethany and Cliff, a question: "Will you nurture Gabrielle in Christ's holy Church, that by your teaching and example, she may be guided to accept God's grace for herself, to profess her faith openly, and to lead a Christian life?" We answered boldly, "We will."

When you develop a faith muscle, you help the next generation do it because of their association with you. One of the reasons that we asked Bethany and Cliff to be Gabrielle's godparents is because we know the power of their faith muscles. Their stories, and now *your* stories, become important to how those coming behind you will act out their faith.

Chapter Takeaways

Now that you know a lot more about my faith journey and what it takes to build a faith muscle, I want you to ask yourself two questions:

- *Are there areas in my life where I allow fear or lack of action to get in the way of my faith?*
- *How can I use the strategies that I just learned to build my own faith muscle?*

Step 7: Be a Girl

Now that you have gone through six steps to becoming a Wealthy Girl, let's take that next *big* step. I know you will embrace this seventh step because it is part of who you already are in your life. But start first to honor the definition of "girl" that you ascribe to yourself.

I am a cisgender female. If you are not familiar with the definition of "cisgender," it is the gender you were identified with at your birth. Growing up, I liked playing with trucks more than dolls. Today, I like dresses as much as sweatpants. I prefer dancing in flats over heels any day. I love sports as much as I love cooking a Sunday meal for my family. I choose to pay a female small business owner to clean my house every other week. I hate shopping for clothes if it takes more than thirty minutes, but I love to adorn myself in form-fitting outfits to accentuate my figure. I like going to brunch with my girls when the opportunity affords.

I negotiate hard and ask for the money I want. I am incredibly grateful to my husband for taking out the garbage 98 percent of the time, always mowing our lawn, and getting our cars fixed. I love mothering my daughter Gabrielle. Finally, my gender identity is female. I prefer the pronouns she/her/hers when you speak to me.

I recognize the role that societal expectations and cultural norms play in the social construction of gender. I first understood the complexities of gender identity and gender expression as an American studies major at Yale, where I also studied how gender intersects with race and class. There is plenty of research that provides insight into the full range of gender identity and gender expression definitions.[69] These definitions are complicated and ever evolving as our society grapples with the reality that you cannot place people in a box that is sometimes incongruent with how they see themselves.

Suppose you are gender nonconforming, transgender, or choose to identify yourself differently. In that case, my goal in this chapter is to harness the beauty of whatever manner you choose to define yourself.

After you honor the "girl" in you, as defined by you, I want you to understand that there is power in the unique way girls can create wealth for themselves and others. If you remember from Chapter 1, I shared my definition of being a Wealthy Girl. I want to remind you of the core of that now that we're approaching the end of the book.

Being a girl for your purposes is a mind-state which harnesses the power of the collective. I want you to be that girl who has a community-centric mind to enable you to move forward and farther a bit faster in achieving your wealth goals. When you do this, you will allow those around us to benefit as well. Please recall that no one creates real wealth alone, but does so by working with the community around them.

Now I want to share my grandmother's story and how she harnessed her girl power to create wealth for her family. My Grandma Shine migrated north to Harlem, in New York City, in 1949. There she met my grandfather, Joseph, and a year later, they had my mom Barbara, the first of their six children. In 1966, when my mother was sixteen years old, her family went to sleep on Christmas Eve only to be jolted awake in the middle of the night by a fire in their apartment. My grandparents and all six children made it out of that apartment with no physical scars on their bodies, while the apartment was rendered uninhabitable. I do call that a miracle.

My mother and her family found themselves without a place to call home on Christmas Day. My grandmother often tells me how depressed and distraught she felt. My mother has shared with me the details of how the family temporarily split up. Some went to one aunt's house and the rest went to another aunt's house, while my grandmother and grandfather tried to figure out what they were going to do. They all lived apart from each other for a couple of months.

Eventually, my grandparents found an apartment at 425 West 25th Street in Chelsea. If you are unfamiliar with the geography of New York, Chelsea is in the heart of Midtown Manhattan. During the 1960s, Chelsea felt a world away from Harlem, even though it is only a thirty-minute express train ride from downtown.

Chelsea would be my grandparents' home for roughly the next twenty-eight years. The neighborhood is quite different today than it was more than fifty years ago. When my mom and her family moved there, their apartment was situated in the Chelsea-Elliott Houses, a housing project of the New York City Housing Authority. Growing up, everyone called this slew of apartments "The Projects," the slang name given to the government-owned, subsidized housing project for low-income residents.

Whatever name it went by, it did not seem to faze my mother and her siblings. All eight of them were finally reunited in a safe, spacious apartment. Those four bedrooms, two bathrooms, kitchen, dining room, living room, and foyer space became the backdrop of many intergenerational family pictures for years to come. Most of all, the apartment was full of love. They had more than enough love.

In the previous chapter, I wrote about building a faith muscle. I believe that my grandmother's faith muscle helped her withstand the depression that came with the 1966 fire and move forward, hoping for a brighter future.

Grandma Shine got all the things she hoped for, and more. My grandparents' apartment became the center of community, not just for my mom and her siblings, but also for the many relatives and friends. Some would come from the South to the North to stay with them when they made their own Great Migration trek, while other local relatives would simply be given a place to lay their heads in time of need. From the 1970s until my grandparents moved out in 1996, their apartment was the premier gathering spot for over twenty-five family members for Christmas dinners, after-church Easter celebrations, and big birthday bashes.

My grandparents had fourteen grandchildren, and all of us have fond childhood memories of that apartment. Whether my cousin Sonja and I played the game 'spit' in the back bedroom or my brother Clayton shared his rap songs with my cousins, we simply had fun. It was the place to be. I remember never really wanting to be anywhere else. As we squeezed into every nook and cranny when additional family members or friends would show up, there was always enough room to fit everyone. All were welcome.

Grandma Shine often talks about how she wanted her home to be a haven for others. She knew what it was like for others to make room for her and her family, particularly when she got burnt out of her home in 1966. She used her apartment as a communal resource to infuse love, laughter, and as God as my witness, so many delicious home-cooked soul food dishes into the bellies of so many people.

After twenty years of being on the waiting list for a cooperative housing community in the Mutual Redevelopment Houses several blocks away, my grandparents received notice that they were approved and decided to move out of their apartment in early 1996. But Grandpa Joe passed away in September of that year, and my grandmother decided to stay right there. To this day, my family still all squeezes into her much smaller Chelsea apartment, which has a crystal-clear balcony view of Madison Square Garden and the Empire State building.

Grandma Shine is beloved by so many family members to this day because of her keen ability to harness a collective power that cuts across generations. While many ninety-two-year-olds experience a decrease in visits or phone calls as they get up in age, my grandmother seems to get more as she gets older. And no one comes to New York without paying Grandma Shine a visit and picking up food or flowers for her on their way.

Grandma Shine's "power of the collective" approach to life is one of the quintessential elements of being a girl. The community does better when it pools its resources, shares instead of hoards, and makes enough room for others. Grandma Shine embodies what it means to be a true girl. At its essence, "being a girl" means being committed to being there for the community around you.

There is power in a community-centric approach to building wealth. Focusing on the community can accelerate what you are doing as an individual. I've seen it work with my grandmother's life, and I know it can work in yours.

Here's how you can make "being a girl" work for you, and harness its magical power.

Identify Your Girl Superpowers

You should first identify your girl superpower, or the skill sets, talents, or attributes that are uniquely yours and help contribute to your wealth, including the community around you. And then you must leverage those superpowers.

My Grandma Shine leveraged her girl superpowers—cooking, praying, and the gift of honest gab—to infuse life into everyone around her and bring people together for a common purpose.

I'll give you a few additional examples of girl superpowers.

One of my closest friends, Phoebe, has the incredible girl superpower of "the ultimate hustle." I've known Phoebe since I was twelve years old, when we met in the sixth grade in Freeport, New York. Phoebe is one of my Sisters of the Spirit that I mentioned in Chapter 3, and the same one who sent me the encouraging Mother's Day text that I referenced in Chapter 9. Phoebe was born in Jamaica and migrated to Brooklyn when she was six years old, and then her family moved to Freeport when she was twelve. Phoebe and I went to junior high school and high school together, and spent countless hours together after college when we both settled back in New York.

As long as I've known Phoebe, she has been resourceful. She is typically a step ahead in thinking about taking advantage of an opportunity or who needs to help get something done. You may have a friend like Phoebe: you tell her that you want to have a party at a restaurant, and within the hour, she provides three concrete recommendations. She also tells you how to get a discount if you make reservations by Thursday. She then helps you create an invite using the latest mobile app.

Your same friend also has a job on the side and has figured out how to make money from a significant market trend. A few years ago, Phoebe bought a house next door to her current residence, convinced her husband to renovate it, and then rented the house on Airbnb after recognizing that she could get premium value. Phoebe's ultimatehustle girl superpower came to life, too, when she launched a website to sell masks for children and adults out of her home at the onset of the COVID-19 pandemic. More inspiring, Phoebe applies her "the ultimate hustle" girl superpower in the daily grind of mothering her three boys, including a set of twins.

My Aunt Melissa embodies another example of a girl superpower: visualization. Aunt Melissa is more like an older sister to me; we are separated by twenty-three years, but she physically looks like she is only ten years older than me. She is a visual person. While she appreciates inner beauty, she has a knack for bringing out the beauty of what you see on the outside. Aunt Melissa puts effort into ensuring that her hair, nails, clothes, and makeup are always put together well. She will always compliment me on my outward appearance, and she provides honest feedback if she believes an outward appearance can be improved.

When I started working at J. P. Morgan in my early twenties, it was my Aunt Melissa who beat into my head how important it was to have an executive presence. She encouraged me to dress for the role I wanted in the future rather than the one I currently possessed. "Appearance matters," as she continues to say to this day. Her visualization superpower also emerges for our family gatherings when she brings fresh flowers to adorn the dinner table, or a beautiful dessert that captures the admiration of the eye and the desire of the belly.

What are your girl superpowers?

If you are unsure of your girl superpower or want to pick up another one, consider adopting this one: "spread the word." This superpower is any easy one for you to make your own. All you have to do is share information, resources, or ideas that are worth spreading. Tell someone else about something that has benefited you or that may benefit someone else. I know you can do this.

When you have identified your girl superpowers, you can channel them into creating wealth for yourself and others. I want to share one powerful way to do so.

Form Wealth Circles and Wealth Pots

Wealth Circles are a very tangible way to work with others toward a common goal of building wealth together. Remember, I told you about the power of informal peer groups back in Chapter 3? Well, Wealth Circles take informal peer groups to a higher level.

There's no better way to grow wealth together than forming circles where you can do so in a very tangible and intangible way. The intangible way is to use your girl superpowers to bring together like-minded individuals to come together around a common goal to achieve wealth. The tangible way is that you pool your money collectively to advance each individual's pursuits, or everyone's together, in the Wealth Circle.

Let me show you an example.

In April 2019, I asked twenty of my family members if they were interested in pooling our dollars together in a Wealth Circle to invest together and educate ourselves on different opportunities to generate returns for our family. Half of the family members wanted to partake in the endeavor, while the other half opted out. In total, we had ten family members and five units, wherein a husband-and-wife team counted as two family members but one unit.

In April 2019, each family unit committed to putting aside $5,000 to invest in an asset class that we would eventually all agree on: real estate, stocks, or a family member's start-up venture. We then decided to give ourselves a year to save up the $5,000. As we built our unit stash of $5,000 throughout the year, we planned to meet once a month on a video call to hold each other accountable, share ideas, and educate ourselves with our collective experiences.

Fast forward twelve months to March 2020 and the onset of COVID-19. Each family's circumstances changed, making it difficult for them to part with the $5,000 they had saved for our wealth endeavor. As a group, we decided to "pivot" our strategy. First, several family members recruited three additional family units, and thus we had eight family units. From April to August 2020, we abandoned the initial goal of investing in a particular asset class and refocused our efforts on creating a family Wealth Pot.

The way a Wealth Pot works is simple. Each month, there is a Wealth Pot recipient who is entitled to the agreed-upon money collected from the other family units. In our Wealth Pot, each month every unit except the unit receiving the funds that month contributes $500. Thus, each month a different family recipient will get $3,500. Since there are eight family units, the Wealth Pot is scheduled to last for eight months with each unit receiving the pot once.

In my example, the $3,500 each family unit gets from the Wealth Pot once is equal to the $500 each unit will put into the pot for the others over the other seven months.

There is no interest at any point, but rather each family unit gets an influx of cash during one month that the unit probably would not be able to put together on their own. So the Wealth Pot is really a forced savings mechanism that supports a group of people's goals at different points over a specified time.

Each family member can do whatever it wants with their Wealth Pot. In our family, these goals have included paying down credit card debt, investing in the stock market, starting a business, and providing a cash cushion so that a family member did not have to immediately return to work after maternity leave.

There are several big value propositions to Wealth Pots. The first is that money stays within the Wealth Circle community to advance the goals of its members. Secondly, the pooling and redistribution of money helps the wealth circle members get a windfall of money at a specified point in time. Lastly, there can be an extreme financial benefit when the numbers get large enough, which means higher windfalls of cash.

Now, one downside to Wealth Pots is if any members defect or choose not to pay in. If a member fails to contribute to the Wealth Pot, the other members suffer. As such, the success of the Wealth Pot is contingent on each member meeting their responsibilities. Once a member fails to do so, trust is broken, and the other members will be short of money.

For these reasons, I am a big proponent of closed Wealth Pots with a finite number of people who you know. For one, it preserves a level of intimacy, and two, these circles are ultimately built on trust. And I believe strongly that trust is reserved for the people that have earned your trust and you know where and how to find them if something goes wrong. In my Wealth Pot, one of the underlying motivations for each member to pay on time is a shared personal commitment to the other group members. And, if anyone defects, they know that it will be embarrassing to engage with the others in other aspects of their relationship if they owe them money.

You can use several tactics to ensure the success of payment and the Wealth Pot. You should honestly discuss and agree on who needs or has a desire to get the money first and who can wait until later in the payment cycle. Determine what the schedule is going to be up front and stick to it. You should also have an easy way to send the money to each recipient. In the absence of physically providing cash to members, mobile payment apps are a reliable resource to facilitate funds transfer.

You should also affirm that everyone is comfortable putting in the agreed amount of monthly payment, whether $500 or $5,000. Finally, I highly recommend that you establish official documentation of the rules of engagement, with each person committing to the rules in writing. You can document the payment terms and processes, what happens if a member does not pay into the Wealth Pot, the penalties for late or missing payment, and each member's expectations.

The Wealth Pot concept is not new nor complicated. In fact, it should sound somewhat familiar. In essence, the Wealth Circle has created an unofficial, non-interest-bearing bank for its members using the Wealth Pot as a mechanism to provide money when needed. The Wealth Circle dictates its own terms, preventing any of its members from jumping through hoops to access money or prove their worth to a traditional financial institution where they have no intimate relationship.

Again, the Wealth Pot basis is trust established by members of the Wealth Circle who want to see each member succeed. It's a powerful way to provide capital for members to take advantage of opportunities on their own terms.

It is not surprising, then, that the Wealth Pot concept can be traced to communities that have been locked out of traditional financial systems. During the late 1700s, which was smack in the middle of American chattel slavery, "free Black businessmen relied on their own race for capital. Black banking was a private affair."[70]

Prominent Black clergy and business owners formed mutual aid societies to support their own community's goals, as described in Mehrsa Baradaran's *The Color of Money: Black Banks and the Racial Wealth Gap*. Baradaran provides details on the Reconstruction era, or the time period immediately following emancipation from slavery,

"Black communities formed hundreds of mutual aid societies to work toward economic self-sufficiency."[71]

The Wealth Pot structure also reflects the Ujamaa principle, which is based on cooperative and collective economics. Ujamaa, the Swahili word for extended family, was a social and economic policy developed and implemented in Tanzania by President Julius Kambarage Nyerere between 1964 and 1985.[72] Ujamaa relies on the collective to advance the individual and the individual to advance the collective.

Many Asian immigrant communities use the Wealth Pot concept. In many African and Caribbean cultures, the Wealth Pot is called a *sou sou*. These sou sous operate under the same concept, wherein "they act as a collective savings account that is rotated among trusted family members or friends."[73] I have many Caribbean friends whose families have benefited from sou sous throughout their entire childhood, and who as adults are now members of their own sou sous.

In the COVID-19 era, there was an explosion of "Blessing Looms," which are illegal pyramid schemes. On the surface, they sound similar in concept to a Wealth Pot or sou sou. However, there are major differences. These Blessing Looms promise a return for starters or a promise to pay you back more than your initial contribution. Furthermore, Blessing Looms are not closed to a finite number of people; they rely on each member to get other members to join over time, and for the total membership to keep increasing. These types of arrangements are illegal, and the people who promote them are trying to scam you. Beware please!

That said, I want you to strongly consider forming Wealth Circles, where you can leverage the collective superpowers of the individual members to advance the whole group. And, when the right combination of girls get together to form Wealth Circles, good things are bound to happen. While you may use your Wealth Circles to create Wealth Pots and pool your dollars, that's not the only way to make use of Wealth Circles. You should also use Wealth Circles to save money toward a common tangible goal, share valuable information, educate each other on various financial and non-financial opportunities, and hold each other accountable to each other's goals.

As you think about creating your own Wealth Circle, think about inviting people who you can trust. Organizing Wealth Circles requires hard work up front, but the longterm benefits will outstrip those initial efforts once you establish a strong foundation. And guess what? I suspect you will also have a lot of fun in the process of creating wealth for not only yourself but those around you and coming after you.

Get the Men Involved and Committed

If you're going to have longevity in pursuing your wealth goals, you must get the men in your life involved and committed to supporting you. Being a girl means harnessing the collective power of that other species: the dudes. Men are important allies and contributors to the wealth you want to have. Invite the men to your Wealth Circles and contributors to your Wealth Pots if they have similar values and help move forward the group with real dollars.

When I think back to the many opportunities I've had to build intangible wealth over my life, the men have played their own unique role. Growing up, my dad and brother always found a way to help instill confidence in me by complimenting me on how I looked, what I wore, and my book smarts. Their compliments helped me overcome the self-doubt that sometimes crept into my psyche because of something I mentioned way back in Chapter 1: strabismus. I'll dive deeper now.

Strabismus, or "crossed eyes," occurs when both eyes do not line up in the same direction due to a weakness in the muscles around the eye and the brain's inability to see two aligned images. Strabismus prevents both my eyes from looking at the same object at the same time. I neither read with both eyes, nor have the ability to see in 3D, given a lack of depth perception due to the condition. When I was a child, I often had to overcome ridicule and work extra hard to believe that I belonged.

Even though I've had three surgeries on my eyes to correct the alignment in my eyes, they can still wander from time to time. I started wearing glasses at age one to prevent me from going blind, and I have continued to wear glasses and contacts into adulthood to help my vision.

Growing up, however, I never felt abnormal for very long because the men in my life affirmed my inner and outer beauty despite my strabismus. These men helped to add tremendous intangible wealth to my life, in the form of my sense of self and belonging.

Research suggests that when fathers are supportive of their children, children have higher self-esteem.[74] The confidence I gained from my father's support has stayed with me through adulthood, and it has surely helped me to take more risks. As I mentioned in Chapter 6, confidence is a key factor in developing an investor mindset, and my father had a direct role in developing mine.

Are there men in your life who have helped create attributes in you that have helped you be wealthy? What are those attributes, and who have those men been? If not, are there men who could serve as allies to help you achieve your wealth goals?

Sometimes, however, men need to be asked for their support or guidance because it's not readily offered. The first step is to communicate what you need, which can be easier said than done. If you don't ask, you will not get. Given that we still live in a patriarchal society, you must continue to ask for what you need often. Keep in mind, however, that asking politely may not always work. I want you to get comfortable asserting yourself to take hold of things you want. If you need to ask your partner to do more around the house, take on more of the child-rearing responsibilities, or stop working so you can advance in your career, ask.

And if asking doesn't work, I want you to demand what you need. You sometimes need to insist on what you need and perhaps even give an ultimatum. You can say, "If you cannot support me in this way, these are the consequences." You need to do this for the sake of your family and your community and be willing to sometimes walk away if those demands are not met. Stand in your truth and honor thyself.

For instance, you may need your husband to watch the kids while you work on your new business idea or project. You may need to demand your male colleagues to shut up and listen and allow the women to speak first in meetings. You may need to demand a higher salary or promotion from the men around you.

Finally, I want you to receive the help that men provide. If you're like me, the art of receiving can be difficult. I have problems receiving the help. Over the years, I've learned that it's undoubtedly okay to say "yes" to help, and then I pray that God helps me receive it with a smile. Over time, I have learned to say "thank you" and keep it moving. There is power in receiving what's being given to you with gratitude and absolutely no regrets.

Men can play a special role in your efforts at being a girl. Let them in when they offer, and demand their support when they don't.

Chapter Takeaways

I think back to my Grandma Shine and how desperate she must have been standing outside her burning apartment in Harlem in 1966. She eventually received helping hands from other women and men in the community invested in her family's survival. Grandma Shine learned from that experience, and in the process developed the girl super-powers that still reside in her today. These super-powers have created prosperity, peace, and personal power for her family. They inspire me to have my own.

As a girl, you, too, have unique girl superpowers to build the wealth you want to see in your life. In essence, your Wealthy Girl mojo is manifested due to what lays within you and then can be unleashed externally. I have shared the benefit of forming Wealth Circles and Wealth Pots as powerful examples of applying that mojo.

The actions you take now will flow to the next generation of individuals and their wealth pursuits. My Grandma Shine always tells me, "Do you know why people die, Charisse? Because the next generation needs the room to grow and to leave their mark on the world. Life is better because we have the next generation." Her philosophy is that the older generation has to make way for the upcoming ones so they don't wind up living in a shadow.

The way in which you can set the next generation up for a wealthy life is to be the girl in you. I challenge you with one last thought:

As you think about the generation above you and the one below you, how you can be that girl who builds wealth for those around you?

And that, my friend, will take you on a life-giving journey of being a Wealthy Girl.

11

Enjoy Your Wealth: Prosperity, Peace, and Personal Power Lived Out

I WANT TO ENSURE THAT you have everything you need to be the Wealthy Girl I know that you can be, and that you already are.

This last chapter is about embracing the prosperity, peace, and personal power that come from your efforts toward building a wealthy life. So it's about living into and enjoying your wealth. Wealth is personal, as I've explained throughout this book. I have also shown you *how* to attain wealth over the last ten chapters. And I have wonderful news: your personal enjoyment of wealth is just as important as attaining it.

Isn't this the point of building wealth anyway?

I've been fortunate to have many wealthy moments in my life, and those are captured in the daily waking up, seeing my family joyful, and building the relationships that make life more abundant. My wealthy moments are also captured in the birthdays, trips, and milestones that often come with celebration. When I see my bank account grow, make money from my investments, or successfully execute in my entrepreneurial ventures, I am wealthy too.

These wealthy moments, when strung together, create a wealthy life. Your wealthy life is rooted in a wealthy mindset, which is what being a Wealthy Girl is all about. I am confident that your wealthy life will manifest itself in the way you want it to if you follow the steps that I have shared with you.

I want you to enjoy all of your wealthy moments. Which moments stick out to you, or do you want to strive toward? One wealthy moment I enjoyed immensely was my trip to the Philippines with my mother, father, and brother. The trip gave me prosperity, peace and personal power. As I mentioned back in Chapter 1, my paternal grandfather was from the Philippines. In an attempt to find out more about my Filipino roots and understand more about the other side of my family, we all decided to make the trek to my grandfather's first home. Thus, the trip represented a quest for my full identity.

We had always talked about traveling together outside of the States, and this was our first opportunity to do so. As such, we had decided a year prior to save up enough money to cover our flight, hotel, food, and other trip expenses. We each planned to save approximately $3,000, especially since the flight alone would cost $1,500, even with a discounted rate on Singapore Airlines where one of my Philippines-based cousins worked. Saving up $3,000 was achievable since we each saved $250 per month for an entire year. Our ability to save enough money ahead of our trip would prevent us from having any unpaid outstanding balances on our credit cards when the trip was over.

Given the significance of the trip, several of my Filipino cousins who had immigrated to the U.S. in the 1990s decided to join us. My cousins served as our personal escorts to help us experience the Philippines for the first time under their guidance, and through their native eyes. We decided to go in August 2008, a month before I was heading to Chicago to go to business school.

A month before our departure, we decided to appropriate our trip for a dual celebration. First, we wanted to celebrate my father's retirement from twenty years of teaching home instruction for special education students in New York City. Second, we wanted to celebrate my acceptance into Chicago Booth. I was ready to celebrate because I got a full scholarship from Amy and Richard Wallman, who endowed two scholarships per year to women based on their academic performance.

After our eighteen-hour flight, we stepped off the plane in Manila to see three of my Filipino cousins waiting for us at the gate. Our arrival was met with the kind of embrace that one could only dream about when being welcomed in a country that was not *yet* our own. By the time we left, we felt that it *was* our own.

We stayed in Manila for a few days and then all flew to the island of Aklan, a half-hour plane ride south of Manila, where my grandfather and his siblings grew up. The family still owned the house of my grandfather's brother, my Uncle Jimmy, who passed away in 1992. As we drove up the street named "Conanan," our eyes widened as we saw a huge sign on the front of the house that read "Welcome, Conanan Family!" The Conanan last name is quite popular in the Philippines, a stark contrast to the low number of people familiar with the Filipino origin of Conanan in the United States.

Seeing the enshrined "Welcome, Conanan Family" against the wall helped us embrace our full identity. It absolved us from feeling anxious about fitting in. It provided a sense of peace because it allowed us to return to our roots in such a smooth way, far exceeding our expectations and quelling our fears.

There was no replacement for standing in the home where my forefathers were born. To our surprise, there were childhood pictures of my brother and me as well as pictures of my mother and father as young adults all over the house. Apparently my Grandma Pearl had been sending these pictures back to the family on my grandfather's behalf for years. You must remember that sending these pictures internationally took herculean effort as there was no internet back then, when things traveled by snail mail.

I share this wealthy moment in light of the prosperity utilized to make this trip happen, the peace gained from discovering a missing part of my identity, and the personal power obtained from pursuing what I wanted with my family. There's no substitute for enjoying the wealth that comes with experiences like the one I had. You too can enjoy the wealthy experiences and opportunities that are uniquely yours. They may enhance who you are as an individual, or fulfill the dreams that you want to pursue.

Whatever form they take, enjoy them.

Final Tips for Your Journey

I want to leave you with a couple of tips for your journey. First, you might not feel compelled to search for an identity on the other side of the world like I did. You don't have to go across the world to find wealth for yourself. Mine happened to be across the world, and it was important for me to personally be there, especially given the technologically advanced world that we inhabit. You might have something else you have been wanting to do for a long time. Or it may take you some time to truly reflect on what this might be for you.

I talked about journaling back in Chapter 5, wherein you put pen to paper for your ideas and dreams. What is one dream that you'd like to pursue that allows you to enjoy your wealth? I encourage you to take a few minutes to write about that right now.

Second, share your dreams with others. It's so important to share those wealth dreams with others who might also have very similar wealth dreams. I shared my dream to travel to the Philippines with my mother, father, and brother. We started talking about it, then wrestling with it, and then eventually affirming each other's ability to make it happen. Sharing your dreams with others is a key component of enjoying wealth.

Third, put forth the dollar investment that makes enjoying your wealth possible. Sometimes you must make sacrifices to set aside money to pursue these dreams. But that will no longer be an issue since you will develop an investor mindset, which I talked about in Chapter 6. Remember that you are the CEO of your wealth, and it's imperative that you set the vision, stay action-oriented, and build confidence. I've talked about investing in those big things in your life, and not sweating the small stuff, like the lattes and the teas. Your dreams are big and it often takes money to achieve them; achieving these big dreams is doable with your investor mindset. So, ask yourself, "What should I do with my money in order to invest in my dreams?" Or, "how can I make the SIPPin' & Livin' allocation strategy work for me to pursue my dreams?" Whatever approach you take, stick with it and stay focused on the dream.

Putting aside dollars to enjoy your wealth means leveraging continued financial prosperity.

Prosperity Lived Out

I pose to you: who doesn't like seeing their bank account go up in value? In my discussion with thousands of women, I have yet to meet a person who does not want to see more money in their bank account. Part of enjoying your wealth means letting your tangible wealth work for you. Having continued financial prosperity will not be so hard if you put into practice the steps that I've talked about.

As your tangible wealth grows, it becomes easier to take advantage of opportunities because you have a little more at your disposal. You may enjoy access to exclusive financial products that come along with simply having more dollars. For instance, you may be able to invest in more stocks and ETFs at lower trading fees, or get access to financial products (e.g., mortgages, lines of credit, etc.) that have lower rates. Or you may enjoy benefits that come in the form of opportunities to earn extra income because you can now invest in a career-accelerating training or certification, or invest in a business—your own or someone else's.

But again, financial prosperity is not the only way to be wealthy. You can also have nonfinancial prosperity, which I have been calling intangible wealth throughout the book. Enjoyment comes with being healthy. It's hard to enjoy anything if you are physically unwell. Also, your emotional and spiritual well-being are at the center of your enjoyment as they provide liberation to your mind and soul to actually enjoy your circumstances. As such, you should make your physical health, emotional, and spiritual well-being a priority.

Some people call the prioritization of your well-being self-care, while others call it investing in yourself first. However you want to frame it, make your prosperity work for you and enjoy it.

Peace Lived Out

Enjoying your wealth is also about taking in peace. I've talked about different ways to bring in peace, such as building a faith muscle in Chapter 9. You must also remove things and people that distract you from that peace. This is critical to enjoying your wealth. For me, when I decided to travel to the Philippines before starting business school, several people said to me, "You're going to take that trip right before you start school? Don't you need to prepare and spend time bonding with your classmates?"

I said to them, "Well, taking this trip will actually give me the peace I need to get off to a good start at business school. I'll have plenty of time to bond with my classmates later." If you find yourself in a situation where people are telling you things that distract you from how *you* want to enjoy your wealth, they're just not the right people to surround yourself with. Define what success means for yourself and have no regrets about your decisions. You can do this by creating a wealthy environment, as we discussed in Chapters 3 and 4, with your family, friends, and A-Team.

Another way to take in peace, and thus enjoy your wealth, is by lessening the fear and anxiety that often creeps into our daily lives. In 2020, we looked no further than COVID-19 to bring out our worst daily fears. Fear also emerges when you feel like you're not going to have enough or that the money in your bank account will not meet your financial needs. Your fear may take the form of not knowing how your rent or mortgage will get paid if you lose your job. Your anxiety may take hold when you realize that your employer-sponsored health insurance may not cover a medical procedure you need to get done. Your fears and anxieties are real and natural. After all, you are human.

Fear and anxiety, however, can be managed and contained. Remember in Chapter 4, where I advised you to invest in a therapist. A good therapist can help you alleviate these real fears and anxieties. Additionally, I lean on two verses from the Bible that have helped many times. Philippians 4:6-7 states: "Do not be anxious about anything, but in every situation, by prayer and petition, with thanksgiving, represent your requests to God. And the peace of God, which transcends all understanding, will guard your hearts and minds in Christ Jesus." As a Christian, I have found real power in these words. Regardless of your religion or spiritual practices, or lack thereof, find words that can speak to you with an authority that can lead to you finding peace.

For instance, in 2019, one of my business coaches forced me to make a positive affirmation that I could use every single day. The affirmation has provided the direction and calmness that allowed me to have peace and actually enjoy the pursuit of my daily activities. My affirmation reads:

> *Lord, let my light shine today. Let my words and my actions be Christlike, and fulfill the purpose that You have for my life. Close the doors that need to be closed, open the doors that need to be opened. Protect my family so that I might see them again.*

My affirmation has provided a guidepost for how I want to live every single day. I still say it to this day. You can choose to also affirm yourself every single day. Feel free to borrow or tweak mine. Feel free to make your own. Ultimately, enjoying your wealth comes with a peace that should remind you that you are a light in this world. And I want you to shine your light brightly.

Personal Power Lived Out

Finally, enjoying your wealth comes from seizing the personal power that you have obtained from following the seven steps that I have laid out in this book. "Be a girl" is my favorite step for enjoying personal power. Personal power means having the freedom and agency to dictate how you want to live your life on your own terms. Your personal actions matter, even as you exist in a larger system that may indeed be stacked against you.

Successful South African entrepreneur Vusi Thembe-kwayo said it best: "Every single excuse I have is valid, and that's not going to get me the results I want."[75] In his statement, Thembekwayo honors the ways in which apartheid, for example, is a very valid excuse that has affected his actions. At the same time, he does not let apartheid define his existence. If his message doesn't imbue personal power, I don't know what does.

I have talked about how the systems and structures that are in force in American society as well as around the globe. These are real and play into who has power and how doesn't have power. But, when you decide to adopt the Wealthy Girl mantra, your personal power begins to coexist within those systems and structures and I believe, trumps what those systems and structures sometimes try to prevent you from doing.

You can exert personal power by forming Wealthy Girl circles and informal peer groups, and hacking the system with tested strategies to build tangible wealth. In fact, it's your personal power that fights against, and eventually changes, the boundaries that those systems and structures try to put around you.

And the enjoyment that you get because of your personal power translates into personal freedom. The freedom to travel. The freedom to pursue the joy you desire. The freedom to vote. The freedom to love whom you want. The freedom to give and donate to causes that inspire you. The freedom to work as much or as little as you like.

The freedom to spend time as you wish and desire. The freedom to say no. And the freedom to say yes. Shonda Rhimes in her book *Year of Yes: How to Dance It Out, Stand in the Sun and Be Your Own Person* reminds us that saying yes to the things that are important to you is just as important as saying no.[76]

So enjoying your wealth means that you seize that personal power and that you honor the ways in which your personal power affords you freedom, affords you independence, and affords you the ability to put a smile on your face. It's your personal power that gives you the confidence to be who you are, to live into your purpose, and to be the Wealthy Girl that I know you are meant to be.

Chapter Takeaways

The way you live your life matters, and no one is going to do that better than you. So if you're going to enjoy your wealth, make sure you take in prosperity, peace, and personal power. You have to make a decision every single day to embrace these life-giving attributes.

Remember the questions I posed at the very beginning of the book? If not, let me remind you:

Imagine that you are standing in front of a mirror saying, "I am a Wealthy Girl."

How would you feel when you say these words out loud? What is the expression on your face? Do you truly believe in the power of your own words?

Well, you are that Wealthy Girl *now*, so say "I am a Wealthy Girl" proudly and confidently. You are armed with the seven steps to assume your rightful place in the world, and you can enjoy your wealth. If you get discouraged, revisit the steps to encourage you along the way.

Onward you go!

Before You Go

IT WAS SUCH AN honor to spend time with you through-out your reading of this book. I'd like to take just a few more minutes to make a request. It's not a large one, and it will spread the wealth to others.

If you enjoyed this book, would you be so kind as to take a moment, go to Amazon, and look up the title, *A Wealthy Girl: 7 Steps to Prosperity, Peace, and Personal Power* and leave a short review? Even if you only had time to go through a couple of chapters you will be able to leave a review and, if you desire, go back later and add to it once you've had a chance to complete the book. Your first impressions are very useful so don't worry if you have only time now to review one or two chapters.

Finally, note that books succeed by the kind, generous time readers take to leave honest reviews. This is how other readers learn about books that are most beneficial for them to buy. You can take part in wealth building in this manner. To this end, I thank you in advance for this very kind gesture of appreciation. It means the world to me.

Acknowledgments

FIRST AND FOREMOST, I thank my Lord and Savior, Jesus Christ. I would not have written this book without the hand of God surrounding me every step of the way.

I also want to thank my daughter, Gabrielle, for inspiring me to write this book and allowing me to escape into the writing abyss without too much of a fuss. Looking at your smile propelled me to finish what I started. You make me wealthy every day. I love you.

I am grateful for my husband, George, for believing in me and encouraging me through the entire writing process. You managed our household with the utmost grace, free of complaint or annoyance. You pushed me to stay awake many nights or get out of bed early to work on what often felt like a never-ending saga. And I will always cherish your technology skills to help me market the book. Your life partnership means the world to me. I love you.

I owe a lifetime of gratitude to my mother Barbara, father Frank, and brother Clayton. Mom, you are my shero. My life is so joyful because of you. Thank you so much for recounting so many of the stories that I shared in this book, as well as all the ones that did not make it into these pages. Thank you for reading the early version and later versions of the book with full excitement and providing constructive edits that only a mother can suggest. Dad, you were the first guy to love me and it shows each day. You have been consistently cheering me on since day one and this book only provided another opportunity to do so. Clayton, thank you for removing the pressure to be anything other than myself. Your laughter and no-stress check-ins gave me the energy I needed. I love you all.

I would not be where I am today had it not been for the Wealthy Girl mojo of Grandma Shine and Grandma Pearl. Thank you for your prayers and strong example of what it means to live a purposeful life, Grandma Shine. Thank you for your caring spirit, which beams down from heaven and lives in me, Grandma Pearl. I love you both.

I'm also immensely grateful for Bethany Gardner for reading the early version of the book with the right combination of objectivity and sisterhood. You made me the right call to get rid of "gal," and I am so thankful that you kept it real. I love you, sis.

I also want to express extreme appreciation to Michelle Pigott for all of the morning accountability writing and encouraging words to keep my head up. You also provided support in the other areas of my life that almost knocked me down. I love you, sis.

I am especially indebted to my uncles, aunts, godmother, grandpas, and cousins for their unconditional love since the day I was born. I am blessed by the support extended to all of my family and friends whose unwavering support helped me stay committed to the goal. To the Conanan, Johnson, English, Gardner, Shine, Mallory, Springer, Berry, Gamby, Brown, Williams, Shields, Wynter, Covenant United Church of Christ, Emmanuel Baptist Church, Black Church at Yale, Urban Village Church, and BPEC (especially Kia, Seyi, and Jamal) tribes, I love you.

I also all appreciate those who gave me detailed and constructive comments on one or more chapters, especially Nancy Alexander, Vanessa Carr, Spencer Lau, and all the members of my launch team. You gave freely of your time to provide feedback and discuss specifics of the strategies and steps I wanted to convey. You urged me to simplify complicated thoughts, pushed me to bring out the point of my stories, and say what I meant. I love you.

I'm also immensely grateful to the creative hands that surrounded me throughout this process. First, to my publisher and editor Melissa Wilson: your guidance, coaching, and experience are priceless. You helped make my words flow smoothly, and you pushed me to dig deep. You had faith in me to tell my story and to audaciously believe that I had something worth sharing when no one else did. And, I'm thankful for my associate editor Cheryl Booth for your research, countless revisions, and affirming words of encouragement. I am grateful to my final proofreader Gretchen Dykstra, whose excellent read of this book ensured that all the edits were made appropriately. And, I cannot forget Ryan Curtis for meticulously editing and producing the audio version of the book. I am also thankful for Mila, my book cover designer; Charissa Johnson, my book cover photographer; Charita Golden, my book cover and ongoing hair stylist; and Kelly Phillips, my book cover makeup artist. You all are not only creatives, but small business owners, and it was a joy to support you as a consumer of your talented services. Thank you for making me look, feel, and sound so wealthy!

I'm so thankful to my Charisse Says community and Next Street family, who allowed me to learn from them, lend my expertise firsthand, and create the space to finish this book in 2020. You helped me to run wealthy experiments, research various concepts, and lead in a way that directly influenced the writing of this book.

Finally, I'm deeply appreciative of all the current and future Wealthy Girls out there. You drive me to step up my game every day.

About the Author

Charisse Conanan Johnson, CFA (chartered financial analyst), is the original Wealthy Girl, who will define what it means to be wealthy for years to come.

Charisse is author of A Wealthy Girl: 7 Steps to Prosperity, Peace, and Personal Power, wealth expert, investor, business strategist, public speaker, and TV personality. She has pursued a life of purpose by investing in financial markets, teaching, building businesses, and stepping out on faith.

Charisse is a managing partner and head of the advisory practice at Next Street, a mission-oriented firm that is mobilizing how its public and private clients provide more capital, customers, and services to entrepreneurs and small businesses that have been systemically held back. She has worked with clients such as the Obama Foundation, City of Columbus, and Walgreens.

She is also the creator of the Charisse Says platform, where she actively blogs and has produced the Charisse Says Show and Charisse Says Online Academy, where she makes investing simple, easy, and fun. Charisse has been featured as a financial expert on TD Ameritrade and Experian and is a financial contributor to the Huffington Post and American Express OPEN Forum. She is also a general partner with Bulldog Innovation Group, a venture fund focused on Yale alums investing in entrepreneurs with a Yale affiliation.

Prior to launching the Charisse Says platform, Charisse was founder and CEO of www.smarteys.com, a web app that helped college grads manage their finances. In her first job after college, Charisse rose to vice president at J. P. Morgan Asset Management in New York City. She conducted stock market research as a generalist, and her research covered 18 percent of the $10 billion J. P. Morgan Mid Cap Value Fund.

A graduate of Yale University and the University of Chicago Booth School of Business, Charisse loves building relationships, traveling, sports, and exploring the world through international cuisine. She resides in Chicago with her husband, George, and daughter, Gabrielle.

Notes

[1] Ari Shapiro, "'The Color of Law' Details How U.S. Housing Policies Created Segregation," NPR, May 17, 2017, https://www.npr.org/2017/05/17/528822128/the-color-of-law-details-how-u-s-housingpolicies-created-segregation.

[2] MacKenzie Scott, "116 Organizations Driving Change," *Medium,* July 28, 2020, https://medium.com/@mackenzie_scott/116-organizations-driving-change-67354c6d733d.

[3] Juliana Menasce Horowitz, Ruth Igielnik, and Rakesh Kochhar. "Trends in Income and Wealth Inequality," Pew Social Trends, January 9, 2020, https://www.pewsocialtrends.org/2020/01/09/ trends-in-income-and-wealth-inequality.

[4] Isabel V. Sawhill and Christopher Pulliam, "Six Facts about Wealth in the United States," Brookings, June 28, 2019, https://www. brookings.edu/blog/up-front/2019/06/25/six-facts-about-wealth-inthe-united-states/

[5] Robin Bleiweis, "Quick Facts About the Gender Wage Gap," Center for American Progress, March 24, 2020, https://www.americanprogress.org/issues/women/reports/2020/03/24/482141/quick-facts-gender-wage-gap/.

[6] Bleiweis, "Quick Facts."

[7] Kristen McIntosh, Emily Moss, Ryan Nunn, and Jay Shambaugh, "Examining the Black-White Wealth Gap," Brookings, February 27, 2020, https://www.brookings.edu/blog/up-front/2020/02/27/examining-the-black-white-wealth-gap/.

[8] Bell Hooks, *Ain't I a Woman: Black Women and Feminism* (Boston South End Press, 1981).

[9] "Anti-Racism Crossroads Training," Crossroads, accessed November 1, 2020, https://crossroadsantiracism.org

[10] Maggie Potapchuk, Sally Leiderman, Donna Bivens, and Barbara Major, "Flipping the Script: White Privilege and Community Building," Annie E. Casey Foundation, accessed December 29, 2020, https://www.aecf.org/resources/flipping-the-script-white-privilege-and-community-building/.

[11] Margalit Fox, "Katherine Johnson Dies at 101; Mathematician Broke Barriers at NASA," *New York Times*, February 24, 2020, https://www.nytimes.com/2020/02/24/science/katherine-johnson-dead.html

[12] Katty Kay and Claire Shipman, "The Confidence Gap," *Atlantic*, August 26, 2015, https://www.theatlantic.com/magazine/archive/2014/05/the-confidence-gap/359815/.

[13] AFS-USA, "Individualism & Collectivism," Culture Points, AFS-USA, accessed August 20, 2020, https://www.afsusa.org/study-abroad/culture-trek/culture-points/culture-points-individualism-and-collectivism.

[14] CBC Radio. "Venus and Serena's Father Richard Williams on Raising Champions." CBC Radio, accessed September 3, 2020, https://www.cbc.ca/radio/q/schedule-for-wednesday-nov-12-2014-1.2926142/venus-and-serena-s-father-richard-williams-on-raising-champions-1.2926145.

[15] Tina Chang, "Shellye Archambeau, on Being Unapologetically Ambitious," Thrive Global Community, September 9, 2020. https://thriveglobal.com/stories/shellye-archambeau-on-being-unapologetically-ambitious/.

[16] Coach Hub, "Rethink People Development," Coach Hub, accessed September 12, 2020, https://coachhub.io/?gclid=EAIaIQobChMI36L8tdHk6wIVcSatBh2-rgpGEAEYASAAEgKeifD_BwE.

[17] Career Wave. "What Is 'Digital Coaching' Anyway?" Career Wave, accessed September 12, 2020, https://www.careerwave.me/what-is-digital-coaching-anyway.

[18] Brené Brown, *Rising Strong: How the Ability to Reset Transforms the Way We Live, Love, Parent, and Lead* (New York: Random House, 2017).

[19] CFA Institute, "1963 2019A Candidate Examination Results," CFA Institute, accessed November 20, 2020, https://www.cfainstitute.org/-/media/documents/support/programs/cfa/cfa-exam-results-since-1963.ashx.

[20] K. Anders Ericsson, Michael J. Prietula, and Edward T. Cokely, "The Making of an Expert," *Harvard Business Review*, accessed September 21, 2020, https://hbr.org/2007/07/the-making-of-an-expert.

[21] Strategies for Influence, "Malcolm Gladwell: 10,000-Hour Rule," Strategies for Influence, accessed September 21, 2020, https://strategiesforinfluence.com/malcolm-gladwell-10000-hour-rule.

[22] Cal Newport, "Deep Work: Rules for Focused Success in a Distracted World." Cal Newport, accessed June 23, 2020, https://www.calnewport.com/books/deep-work/.

[23] Brigid Schulte, "A Woman's Greatest Enemy? A Lack of Time to Herself," *Guardian,* July 21, 2019, https://www.theguardian.com/commentisfree/2019/jul/21/woman-greatest-enemy-lack-of-time-themselves.

[24] National At-Home Dad Network. "Statistics on Stay-At-Home Dads." At Home Dad, accessed June 23, 2020, https://www.athomedad. org/media-resources/statistics/.

[25] Herminia Ibarra, Deborah Tannen, Joan C. Williams, and Sylvia Ann Hewlett, *HBR's 10 Must Reads on Women and Leadership* (Boston: Harvard Business Review Press, 2019).

[26] Derek Silva, "Robert Kiyosaki: Everything You Need to Know," Smart Asset, March 18, 2020, https://smartasset.com/retirement/robert-kiyosaki.

[27] Robert Kiyosaki, "The Six Basic Rules of Investing," Rich Dad, January 21, 2020, https://www.richdad.com/six-basic-rules-of-investing.

[28] Freddie Mac, "Family Budget Burdens Squeezing Housing: Child Care Costs," Freddie Mac Insight, January 7, 2020, http://www.freddiemac.com/research/insight/20200107_family_budget_burdens.page.

[29] WYN Women's Foundation. "Financial Experience & Behaviors Among Women," 2014-2015 Prudential Research Study, accessed

November 20, 2020, https://wnywomensfoundation.org/app/uploads/2019/07/Financial-Experience-Behaviors-among-women.pdf.

[30] Joshua Dietch and Taha Choukhmane, "Auto-Enrollment's Long-Term Effect on Retirement Saving," T. Rowe Price, accessed November 20, 2020, https://www.troweprice.com/financial-intermediary/us/en/insights/articles/2019/q4/auto-enrollment-long-term-effect.dc-resources.html.

[31] Shlomo Benartzi, "How Digital Tools and Behavioral Economics Will Save Retirement," *Harvard Business Review,* December 19, 2017, https://hbr.org/2017/12/how-digital-tools-and-behavioral-economics-will-save-retirement.

[32] Peter Rudegeair, "When Their PPP Loans Didn't Come Through, These Businesses Broke Up with Their Banks," *Wall Street Journal,* July 31, 2020, https://www.wsj.com/articles/when-their-ppp-loans-didnt-come-through-these-businesses-broke-up-with-their-banks-11596205736.

[33] Merriam-Webster. "Experiment." Merriam-Webster Dictionary, accessed July 3, 2020, https://www.merriam-webster.com/dictionary/experiment.

[34] Robert Taibbi, "Experimenting with Your Life," *Psychology Today,* September 21, 2019, https://www.psychologytoday.com/us/blog/fixing-families/201909/experimenting-your-life.

[35] Elahe Izadi, "Ruth Bader Ginsburg's Advice on Love and Leaning In," *Washington Post,* July 31, 2014, https://www.washingtonpost.com/news/post-nation/wp/2014/07/31/ruth-bader-ginsburgs-advice-on-love-and-leaning-in/.

[36] Next Street. "Chicago's Small Business Ecosystem Assessment." Next Street, accessed November 20, 2020, https://nextstreet.com/portfolio/chicago-small-business-ecosystem.

[37] Jeanine Prime and Elizabeth Salib, "The Best Leaders Are Humble Leaders," *Harvard Business Review,* May 12, 2014, https://hbr.org/2014/05/the-best-leaders-are-humble-leaders.

[38] Nicki Lisa Cole, "What Is Cultural Capital? Do I Have It?" ThoughtCo., September 23, 2019, https://www.thoughtco.com/what-is-cultural-capital-do-i-have-it-3026374.

[39] Bureau of the Census, "1990 Census of Population Vermont," Bureau of the Census, accessed November 20, 2020, https://www2.census.gov/library/publications/decennial/1990/cp-1/cp-1-47.pdf.

[40] Jeff Schmitt, "2020 MBAs to Watch: Tierra Evans, Emory University (Goizueta)," Poets & Quants, May 20, 2020, https://poetsandquants.com/2020/05/20/2020-mbas-to-watch-tierra-evans-emory-university-goizueta/?pq-category=students.

[41] Digital Undivided, "Project Diane," Digital Undivided, accessed November 20, 2020, http://www.projectdiane.com.

[42] Peter Bassine, et al., "Big Ideas for Small Business," Big Ideas for Small Business, accessed December 29, 2020, https://www.bigideasforsmallbusiness.org.

[43] Bassine, et al, "Big Ideas for Small Business."

[44] Tomas Chamorro-Premuzic, "Why You Should Become an 'Intrapreneur,'" Harvard Business Review, March 26, 2020, https://hbr.org/2020/03/why-you-should-become-an-intrapreneur.

[45] John Dearie and Courtney Geduldig, Where the Jobs Are: Entrepreneurship and the Soul of the American Economy (Hoboken, NJ: John Wiley and Sons, 2013).

[46] Coop Institute, "The Benefits of Worker Cooperatives," Democracy at Work Institute, accessed November 20, 2020, https://institute.coop/benefits-worker-cooperatives.

[47] Ben Walker, "A Changing World: The Shifting Gig Economy in 2019," Forbes, May 10, 2019, https://www.forbes.com/sites/theyec/2019/05/10/a-changing-world-the-shifting-gig-economy-in-2019/?sh=f9d813e437b3.

[48] Brian K. Bucks, Arthur B. Kennickell, and Kevin B. Moore, "Recent Changes in U.S. Family Finances: Evidence from the 2001 and 2004 Survey of Consumer Finances," Federal Reserve Board, accessed

November 20, 2020, https://www.federalreserve.gov/pubs/bulletin/2006/financesurvey.pdf.

[49] Kauffman Foundation, "2018 National Report on Early-Stage Entrepreneurship," Kauffman Foundation, accessed November 20, 2020, https://indicators.kauffman.org/wp-content/uploads/sites/2/2019/09/National_Report_Sept_2019.pdf.

[50] Bassine, et al, "Big Ideas for Small Business."

[51] Ian Hathaway and Robert E. Litan, "Declining Business Dynamism in the United States: A Look at States and Metros," Brookings Institution, accessed November 20, 2020 https://www.brookings.edu/research/declining-business-dynamism-in-the-united-states-a-look-at-states-and-metros/.

[52] Emin Dinlersoz, "Business Formation Statistics: A New Census Bureau Product that Takes the Pulse of Early-Stage U.S. Business Activity," U.S. Census Bureau, February 8, 2018, https://www.census.gov/newsroom/blogs/research-matters/2018/02/bfs.html

[53] American Express, "The 2019 State of Women-Owned Businesses Report," www.s1.q4cdn.com, accessed November 20, 2020, https://s1.q4cdn.com/692158879/files/doc_library/file/2019-state-of-women-owned-businesses-report.pdf.

[54] American Express, "State of Women-Owned Businesses."

[55] American Express, "State of Women-Owned Businesses."

[56] Bassine, et al, "Big Ideas for Small Business."

[57] Fed Small Business, "2020 Report on Employer Firms: Small Business Credit Survey," Fed Small Business, accessed November 20, 2020, https://www.fedsmallbusiness.org/medialibrary/FedSmallBusiness/files/2020/2020-sbcs-employer-firms-report.

[58] Fed Small Business.

[59] Next Street, "Heard on the Street: Business Roundtable Addresses Racial Injustice, SBA Decreases Loans to Black-Owned Businesses, and More," Next Street, October 19, 2020, https://nextstreet.com/heard-on-the-street-october-19/.

[60] Bassine, et al, "Big Ideas for Small Business."

[61] Amara Omeokwe, "Black-Owned Businesses Hit Especially Hard by Coronavirus Pandemic, Study Finds," *Wall Street Journal,* August 4, 2020, https://www.wsj.com/articles/black-owned-businesses-hit-especially-hard-by-coronavirus-pandemic-study-finds-11596558754.

[62] Board of Governors of the Federal Reserve System, "Report to the Congress on Credit Scoring and Its Effects on the Availability and Affordability of Credit," Board of Governors of the Federal Reserve System, accessed November 20, 2020, https://www.federalreserve.gov/boarddocs/rptcongress/creditscore/creditscore.pdf.

[63] Association for Enterprise Opportunity, "The Tapestry of Black Business Ownership in America: Untapped Opportunities for Success," Association for Enterprise Opportunity, accessed November 20, 2020, https://aeoworks.org/images/uploads/fact_sheets/AEO_Black_Owned_Business_Report_02_16_17_FOR_WEB.pdf.

[64] J. P. Morgan Chase, "Small Business Financial Outcomes during the Onset of COVID-19," J. P. Morgan Chase, accessed November 20, 2020, https://www.jpmorganchase.com/institute/research/small-business/small-business-financial-outcomes-during-the-onset-of-covid-19.

[65] American Express, "State of Women-Owned Businesses."

[66] Kauffman Foundation, "Access to Capital for Entrepreneurs: Removing Barriers," Kauffman Foundation, accessed November 20, 2020, https://www.kauffman.org/wp-content/uploads/2019/12/CapitalReport_042519.pdf.

[67] Melanie Curtin, "73 Percent of Millennials Are Willing to Spend More Money on This 1 Type of Product," *Inc,* March 30, 2018, https://www.inc.com/melanie-curtin/73-percent-of-millennials-are-willing-to-spend-more-money-on-this-1-type-of-product.html.

[68] SMBX, "Become an Investor: Invest and Make an Impact on Small Businesses with the SMBX," SMBX, accessed November 20, 2020, https://www.thesmbx.com/investors.php

[69] American Psychological Association, "Definitions Related to Sexual Orientation and Gender Diversity in APA Documents," American

Psychological Association, accessed November 20, 2020, https://www.apa.org/pi/lgbt/resources/sexuality-definitions.pdf.

[70] Mehrsa Baradaran, *The Color of Money: Black Banks and the Racial Wealth Gap* (Cambridge, MA: Belknap Press of Harvard University Press, 2017).

[71] Baradaran, *Color of Money.*

[72] Alistair Boddy-Evans, "What Was Ujamaa and How Did It Affect Tanzania?" ThoughtCo, August 2, 2019, https://www.thoughtco.com/what-was-ujamaa-44589.

[73] Alexis Johnson, "Investor Beware: Traditional African 'Sou-Sou' Savings Clubs Have Become the Latest Pyramid Scheme," *Pittsburgh Post-Gazette,* August 20, 2020, https://www.post-gazette.com/local/region/2020/08/20/sou-sou-pittsburgh-savings-collective-economics-africa-pyramid-scheme-money/stories/202008190075.

[74] Melanie H. Mallers, Susan T. Charles, Shevaun D. Neupert, and David M. Almeida, "Perceptions of Childhood Relationships with Mother and Father: Daily Emotional and Stressor Experiences in Adulthood," U.S. National Library of Medicine, accessed November 20, 2020, https://www.ncbi.nlm.nih.gov/pmc/articles/PMC3468907

[75] Vusi Thembekwayo, "Is Your Self-Identity Limiting Your Potential?" YouTube, October 6, 2020, https://www.youtube.com/watch?v=Zwk-k4NyO3GA.

[76] Shonda Rhimes, *Year of Yes: How to Dance It Out, Stand in the Sun, and Be Your Own Person* (New York: Simon & Schuster, 2015).

Made in the USA
Middletown, DE
12 February 2021

33686250R00177